DEVELOPING A YOGA HOME PRACTICE

An Exploration for Yoga Teachers and Trainees

Alison Leighton with Joe Taft

Series Editor: Sian O'Neill

SINGING DRAGON
LONDON AND PHILADELPHIA

First published in Great Britain in 2022 by Singing Dragon,
an imprint of Jessica Kingsley Publishers
An Hachette Company

1

A CIP catalogue record for this title is available from the
British Library and the Library of Congress

ISBN 978 1 78775 704 2
eISBN 978 1 78775 705 9

Printed and bound in Great Britain by CPI Group

Jessica Kingsley Publishers' policy is to use papers that are natural, renewable and recyclable
products and made from wood grown in sustainable forests. The logging and manufacturing
processes are expected to conform to the environmental regulations of the country of origin.

Jessica Kingsley Publishers
Carmelite House
50 Victoria Embankment
London EC4Y 0DZ

www.singingdragon.com

DEVELOPING A YOGA HOME PRACTICE

Yoga Teaching Guides
As it grows in popularity, teaching yoga requires an increasing set of skills and understanding, in terms of both yoga practice and knowledge. This series of books guides you towards becoming an accomplished, trusted yoga teacher by refining your teaching skills and methods. The series, written by experts in the field, focuses on the key topics for yoga teachers—including sequencing, language in class, anatomy and running a successful and thriving yoga business—and presents practical information in an accessible manner and format for all levels. Each book is filled with visual aids to enhance the reading experience and includes "top tips" to highlight and emphasize key ideas and advice.

in the same series

Qigong in Yoga Teaching and Practice
Understanding Qi and the Use of Meridian Energy
Joo Teoh
Foreword by Mimi Kuo-Deemer
ISBN 978 1 78775 652 6
eISBN 978 1 78775 653 3
Yoga Teaching Guides

Supporting Yoga Students with Common Injuries and Conditions
A Handbook for Teachers and Trainees
Dr. Andrew McGonigle
ISBN 978 1 78775 469 0
eISBN 978 1 78775 470 6
Yoga Teaching Guides

of related interest

Yoga Teaching Handbook
A Practical Guide for Yoga Teachers and Trainees
Edited by Sian O'Neill
ISBN 978 1 84819 355 0
eISBN 978 0 85701 313 2

Yoga Student Handbook
Develop Your Knowledge of Yoga Principles and Practice
Edited by Sian O'Neill
Foreword by Lizzie Lasater
ISBN 978 0 85701 386 6
eISBN 978 0 85701 388 0

CONTENTS

Chapter 1

BEFORE YOU BEGIN

Why a home practice is important

The idea for this book came about as a result of things I wish I had known whilst developing my home practice as a trainee yoga teacher and, once qualified, as a new yoga teacher. During my training, we were very much encouraged to have a home practice, to explore how poses felt in our bodies and to fully understand correct alignment in syllabus poses. However, there was much to learn on the course, and homework to do, making it a challenge to find time to place a significant focus on my home practice beyond the necessities of the course. Perhaps I wasn't present enough. As Thich Nhat Hanh says: "If you love someone, the greatest gift you can give them is your presence."

On reflection, I could have been more present in my home practice, as it would have been a gift to myself. Practicing at home felt like a means to an end rather than being a wholly enjoyable experience. My focus was mainly on learning the alignment of poses. Later, when I started teaching, much of my home practice was taken up with designing sequences to teach rather than being a way to enrich my own yoga practice. I was attending yoga classes to do that.

I wish I had known how to use and develop my home practice as a means to experiment and develop my own personal yoga experience. In later years, when I was practicing solely for myself, I realized that a number of things were beginning to change. First, I felt that my practice really began to deepen. I was able to practice with a greater degree of presence and offer that presence to loved ones in my life. My breathing became more even; it was easier to access the breath in my practice. My strength and flexibility improved. Most of all, I felt that my home practice really informed my teaching. The more I practiced at home for myself, the better my classes became, and my class numbers increased. It felt very empowering.

Being a yoga teacher requires continuing study and practice. Having a home practice is an essential form of self-study that, if you are open to it, reveals teachings about your body, attitudes towards your practice and the connection between your mind, body and breath. Perhaps you can also include a spiritual practice in this list if you have one, or you might find a spiritual practice evolves. A home practice is much more than a tool to improve your physical asana practice. A home practice can become an integral part of your day and it can bring practices learned on your mat out into your daily life.

Perhaps you have fallen out of the habit of having a home practice but want to return to it. Maybe you feel stuck in your practice, with it lacking variety, or you already have a good home practice and want to build on it. This book aims to inspire you to develop a home practice that is nourishing, experiential and a place from which your own style of yoga can evolve. It is not a guide to alignment of poses; there are many resources that can help with that. Instead, the book aims to complement what you have learned on teacher training courses and provide you with a different perspective on having a home practice.

How to use the book

You should regard each chapter in this book as a layer in the development of your home practice. Each chapter or layer builds on the previous one. The book begins by exploring the gift of presence and then goes on to review basic concepts in Chapter 2, which are then developed, exploring the magic of the breath, breath-inspired movement, the power of intention, energetics and connecting with your creativity to find new shapes and transitions. Basic concepts in your home practice are expanded into a journey of exploration. The aim is to spark curiosity and creativity and to make your practice an immersive and rewarding experience.

It is also possible to use the book in a flexible way, so if you prefer to dip into specific chapters then you will be able to do this without having worked through some of the previous chapters.

Use the book over time. Dip into the book, leave it and then come back to it again. Don't rush the development of your home practice; let it simmer and evolve.

What is a home practice and what is needed?

A home practice is when you practice alone at home or in another space, without being led by another, and create your own practice. It may be a practice of focusing on the breath or a mediation and/or a physical practice of asana. The point of a home practice is that it is your creation and exploration.

Practicing in the community of a group class is wonderful. Community is important, and aspects of a class may spark your imagination and get you practicing something you might not ordinarily think to practice at home. Draw inspiration from a class and then explore it further in your home practice. Practicing in a class and at home complement one another.

You need time and space for a home practice. You might feel that carving out time for your practice takes some effort, but if your practice becomes nourishing and enjoyable, you are likely to prioritize it just as you might if you go to a group class. If time is a challenge, make your home practice a short one, perhaps just ten to fifteen minutes. Your practice could even consist of breath-work alone. Being able to practice when you need to is a powerful tool to have in your life. Or you might be someone who prefers to practice at a regular time; that's something that may feel very healthy for you to do.

Finding space for a home practice can be a challenge too, especially if you are surrounded by family. You need to be able to find a space free of interruptions. That might involve setting some boundaries with others in your home or finding an alternative space to use outside of your home. In terms of physical space, you need space for a mat (or the equivalent amount of space, as a mat isn't always necessary). A small area of wall, clear of furniture, is useful, along with some yoga props. Two yoga bricks, a yoga strap and four to five foam blocks are great to have.

Music, candles and incense are other things you might like to use to accompany your home practice. Identify any other things that might help you to feel motivated to practice. For example, music inspires me to move, so I create playlists of yoga-style music to listen to when practicing. I will also practice outside in the garden if the weather is favorable; this is my favorite place to practice. Many people infuse their space with things that feel special and personal to them, such that the practice and the practice space become a puja, a place of worship. If you are new to creating space, start with putting a plant in the space and treat it well. Honor the plant as you honor the time and space of your practice. Watch both grow. It'll be easier to become present in the space over time.

Before you begin: create presence

Yoga and mindfulness practices are closely intertwined, but it's easy to practice yoga without being mindful of what you are doing. When you first come to your mat when you practice on your own, from what place are you beginning your practice? Why are you practicing yoga today? Is it from a place of necessity, is it for the love of the practice or is it for some other reason? Asking these questions and acknowledging the answers in your mind, whatever they may be, are good mindful practices. They begin to create presence in your practice.

Yoga gives the opportunity to refine your presence. It brings a new level of attention. It's a soft focus where *your presence and attention can be offered to the ones you love.* It is the biggest gift for them and also for you. Being fully present in your practice makes it much more of an immersive experience. Having full awareness of what you are doing and feeling in that moment is information that you can use to build your practice, and this is explored more fully in Chapter 4.

So, what does it mean to be fully present when your head is full of thoughts and your mind is elsewhere? Is it even possible? Being present is about the process of observing and having a high degree of awareness. It means to be truly in the moment, feeling the full sensations of your being. If you can achieve a sense of presence, whether it's for a fleeting moment or for a longer period of time, you may feel at peace, feel happy or have a greater degree of acceptance about something or a situation, for example. *Presence is a gift to yourself as well as to others.* In the context of a yoga practice, you are likely to feel totally in your body and grounded, and you may feel a stronger connection between your body and mind. This is where your mind informs your body, and your body informs your mind.

Being present in the container of a yoga practice is a very good place to start in terms of expanding the concept of presence into your wider life. Being present in your practice will make it feel more embodied and rewarding. These feelings can create a sense of motivation, such that you'll want to return to your home practice time and time again.

There are a number of simple exercises or techniques you can use to create presence in your practice. You might be drawn to one over another or you may want to use a combination of them within a single practice. These practices can be used at any time throughout your practice but you should, at the very least, aim to begin with one of them.

Begin with moments of stillness, dropping into the physicality of your body

Always begin your practice in moments of stillness, whether you are standing, seated or supine, and by taking a few deep breaths. Perhaps close your eyes to aid a feeling of gathering in. Use these quiet moments to drop into your body and focus on physical sensations.

Start by becoming aware of your posture. If seated or standing, check in with how your posture is. Question whether you feel comfortable.

Become aware of the points of contact your body has with your mat. These may just be your feet, or they may also be your seat or the back of your body if you are supine. Focus on the points of contact to create presence.

Touch is a way of dropping into your body, so you might like to place your hands on your body. For example, you can place one hand on your belly and another at your heart center. Use this sense of touch to drop into your body. You will likely become aware of where and how the body moves as you breathe. Use this as a focus for a few breaths.

Tuning into your breath is a way of dropping into your body. You might like to practice some of the breathing techniques that are offered in Chapter 3.

It's possible that your entire practice just consists of moments of stillness. Or you may begin your practice in this way for a period of time that feels right for you. You can also return to using moments of stillness at any time during your practice.

Practice Pratyahara

This is a mindful practice of moving inwards, also known as withdrawing the senses. This is a metaphorical withdrawing of the senses where you consciously block out external sounds and other distractions through concentration and moving within yourself. Below are some techniques that can be used to move inwards. You can practice these with your eyes open or closed.

If you are able to work well with images in your mind, create an image that represents the core of who you are and focus on that image. For example, when I practice in this way, I visualize a seed or a heart shape that sits inside of me. It's an image I create at the start of my practice and return to periodically throughout my practice. You can work with any image that you feel represents the core of you. Just sit quietly, in stillness, and see what image arises. If an image does not arise, create an image to focus on, to draw you inwards, such as a candle flame or the glow of an ember.

If working with an image is not for you, try working with a feeling that draws you inwards. For example, the feeling of warmth throughout your body, a feeling of containment within your body or a sense of peacefulness.

Another way to practice Pratyahara is to visualize the breath moving inside of you as you breathe in. Follow the sense of drawing in to the body both literally (rib cage expands, drawing the air into your lungs) and figuratively (there's an energetic drawing in).

Although Pratyahara is a withdrawal of the senses, the practice of drawing in enables you to observe, listen and sense from within, which is the practice of presence.

Leave your "obstacles" behind

We constantly carry around things we feel burdened by (anxieties, deadlines, pressures, etc.) or are irritated by (issues with relationships, things that haven't been done, lack of sleep, etc.). We also often find reasons not to practice, such as being too busy or having insufficient energy. I refer to these things as "obstacles." These can give you a reason not to get on your mat or act as a distraction once you are on your mat.

By way of your imagination, practice presence by placing your obstacles in an adjacent room with the door closed. You are essentially creating a boundary between your obstacles and your practice. Leave your obstacles there until the end of your practice, at which point you can pick them up again if you choose to. If your obstacles reappear throughout your practice, move them back to where you first placed them. Recommit to placing a metaphorical boundary around your obstacles. This practice is not suggesting you constantly ignore your obstacles; in fact, it is often better to confront them head on. The practice is merely offering a temporary respite from your obstacles, perhaps giving you the insight to deal with them at a later date. You might even find there is a paradox. When you mindfully place your obstacles or your troubles down and then pick them back up, you might see that you are actually holding the solution.

This is not necessarily an easy practice, but it's one to experiment with. You might find that it frees up your practice. If your obstacles involve lack of time and/or fatigue, then practice accordingly. Make it a shorter practice and a softer one, still placing the obstacles away from your mat.

Listen to messages from your body

The body, as opposed to the mind, has an innate intelligence. It sends signals to tell you how you are feeling or it tells you what you might need. A simple example is if your mouth is clenched or your stomach is churning, your body is saying you are tense and nervous. Or some muscles might feel tight, but there is a sense in your body that you need to move in order to reduce the tightness. The body has an amazing capacity to say what it needs or does not need. In your yoga practice, listen for and recognize these messages and then adapt your practice accordingly.

Learn to trust your body to tell you what it needs, but, at the same time, be aware of patterns in your practice that are not optimal for your body. It's possible to become comfortable with practicing postures in a certain way that, although they might feel good now, can harm you over time. This is explored more in Chapter 4.

Practice primarily for yourself, not for others

In your home practice, ensure you spend time practicing for yourself. Tune in to what your body needs. There are days when I do little more than some basic warm-up poses and stretch. There are other days when my practice has a particular focus, such as strengthening posterior chain muscles or working on back extensions. If I'm feeling tired, my practice will be a restorative one. On other occasions, I will move through a full spectrum practice.

Create sequences for yourself that are fun and appeal to you. This book aims to give you the tools to do just that. Inevitably, you will also spend time creating sequences for the classes you teach, but ensure you spend time just practicing for yourself too. Your self-practice sequences are likely to be very different from the sequences you teach in class. They might be more experiential, more advanced or focused on practicing a particular posture.

As you practice for yourself, allow it to be a process of discovery. Regard it as an unveiling.

Intention

Working with a particular intention for a practice is a way to create presence. The intention is set before you practice or as you get on the mat. The aim is to stay with that intention throughout your practice.

The beauty of having an intention is that you get to choose it. Start by setting a simple intention. It could be based on, for example, having a particular anatomical focus for your practice (for example, practicing twists). Or it might be in relation to how you are feeling. For example, you may not feel particularly energized but you know you want to move, so the intention is to explore easy, soft movements where the shapes are created when supine, seated and from a table-top position only (i.e. your practice remains very low to the mat).

Your intention could be to create or practice with a particular feeling. You might want to feel energized or untethered or it could be to practice in an expansive, grounded or light way. An intention could also be something personal, such as sending gratitude to someone who is special in your life. Or it could be to *create the gift of presence so you can later offer it to someone you love.*

The ability to hold an intention requires a consistent focus, which is not easy to achieve. The mind will wander, and you'll likely lose sight of your intention. Returning to your intention, even if only periodically, will form part of creating presence in your practice. The concept of intention and maintaining intention is explored further in Chapter 4.

Practice with caution

Always take steps to keep your practice safe. Listen to your body and don't force it into poses that feel wrong or cause pain. Move into strong poses, or poses practiced for the first time, slowly. Challenging yourself is good provided you keep on the safe side of challenge. Take extra care if you are working with an injury and follow any advice you may have been given by a specialist. If you do injure yourself, it will not be in vain. Use it as an opportunity to deepen your practice and your presence. This is explored further in Chapter 9.

If you are pregnant, please seek advice from your regular teacher for appropriate modifications of your practice and be aware that modifications change throughout different stages of pregnancy.

Summary

- A home practice is your creation and exploration. It differs from practicing in a class or online and from following instructions in a book. A home practice is yours to own.

- Know how and when you are most motivated to practice at home. Make your practice space special to you and practice for a length of time that suits you, even if it's only ten to fifteen minutes.

- Aim to be as present as possible in your practice, and use your practice to cultivate a sense of presence. Presence is a gift. Even if you don't have time to practice physical yoga poses, ten minutes of practicing presence (perhaps while you are traveling) counts as a home practice.

- Take the practice of creating presence on your mat out into your wider life. If you love someone, the greatest gift you can give them is your presence.

Chapter 2

GETTING STARTED

Introduction

This chapter proposes an approach for the first layer of developing your home yoga practice by focusing mainly on your physical practice. This is, after all, the place where most people begin their yoga journey. I like to think of the physical practice of yoga as a way of being in service to my body. This is beautifully and aptly expressed by BKS Iyengar: "My body is my temple and my asanas are my prayers." He describes how the physical practice is a prayer and the body is the temple, a place of worship.

This chapter does not take into account breathing, intention and many other broader concepts. It is simply a place to begin and build on, to develop a deeper yoga experience.

Start by taking a single yoga pose and develop a sequence culminating in that pose. This approach is often taught in yoga teacher trainings, so use it as a first step for building your home practice. You want to be able to move from one pose to the next in a way that flows and is safe for the temple that is your body. In this chapter, sequences are constructed through a process of enquiry regarding areas of the body that need to be warmed up, identifying movements and shapes that support and lead towards that final pose. Although this might seem like a back-to-basics approach, try it. You might make new discoveries by revisiting foundational concepts. It will ignite your home practice. It will certainly invigorate your teaching. Whatever stage you are at in your yoga teaching career, putting small sequences together is a means of exploring movement with your body and connecting to your creativity. From this place, a rich home practice can develop. As your home practice deepens, *your asanas will become your prayers.*

How to form the basics of a sequence

This chapter outlines the approach based on sequencing to a peak or climax pose. There are other types of sequencing, such as having a potpourri of poses, as well as types of yoga that are practiced without heating the body, like yin yoga. Although these approaches are not covered in this book, you might choose to incorporate them as your home practice deepens.

What needs to be warmed up

We spend our waking lives mostly sitting and standing. We are rarely balancing, moving into deep forward folds, twisting or arching the back, as is the case when practicing yoga. Your body is your temple, so move carefully into these non-typical shapes by preparing appropriately through your sequencing.

Take the pose you ultimately want to move into and ask the following questions in relation to what needs to be warmed up.

Weight bearing: Which parts of the body bear weight? We are used to weight bearing on the full soles of our feet, but will other parts of the body bear weight, such as the hands, forearms or head, or will the weight just be placed on one foot or, if on both feet, just on the balls of the feet?

Activation: Which parts of the body need to be engaged and activated as opposed to being softened or relaxed? For example, do one or both legs need to be fully engaged in a posture? Are the arms extended and activated? Consider if any muscle areas need to be strengthened for the final pose.

Mobilization: Which parts of the body need to be mobilized? For example, the spine will need to be mobilized with gentle twists if the final pose is a deep twist. Consider if there are any specific muscle groups that need to be gently stretched, for example, the muscles surrounding the shoulder and upper back for Gomukasana.

Shape: What shape is being created and in what direction? Will the body be twisted or extended backwards? Will certain parts of the body be rotated internally or externally or move sideways?

You might find it helpful to have a visual of the pose to answer these questions. One option is to draw a diagram of the pose using a stick format, as is used throughout this book. You can circle areas of the body where you feel the answers to the above questions are particularly important. These areas of the body can then be warmed up and will form your sequence. This is the approach taken in this chapter.

How to warm up

Once you've identified what needs to be warmed up, the next step is to think about how to warm up. As a general rule, the following guide applies.

Weight bearing: If the pose bears weight on areas of the body that don't normally bear weight, such as the hands, consider whether some preparatory movements to loosen the joints might be appropriate.

Activation: Most yoga poses require activation of the limbs and trunk. Activation exercises are often heating and are therefore good to include in the earlier part of a sequence. For example, if your peak pose is Virabhadrasana 1, consider how you will prepare to activate both the legs and the torso in this pose. The activation of the legs might come from a pointing and flexing of the feet whilst seated in Dandasana. The activation of the torso might come from a focus of drawing the front ribs in whilst in Dandasana and other poses. Breaking a sequence down in this way can bring a positive, detailed focus to your practice as well as to your teaching.

Mobilization: This is an important part of a yoga practice in which areas of the body need to be moved and warmed before creating deeper shapes. For example, the spine will need to be warmed with gentle backbends before moving to a deep backbend like Urdhva Dhanurasana. Similarly, the hamstrings will need to be warmed and stretched if the final pose is a deep forward fold.

Shape: Shapes in poses can often be incorporated in warm-up poses. For example, in Vrksasana the hip of the lifted leg is externally rotated. This external rotation of the hip shape can be incorporated into a warm-up sequence to mobilize the hip joint and surrounding muscles. Exploring shapes in this way, to warm up but also within your practice as a whole, is explored further in Chapter 7.

Constructing a sequence

Once you've identified what needs to be warmed up, you are ready to get on your mat and explore putting a sequence together. The mat is a great place for an enquiry into movement and sequencing; just see where your body takes you. If you prefer, you can create an outline sequence before getting on the mat and then see how it feels once you begin to move. You might like to try both approaches and see which one you prefer.

Below are some guidelines on how you might put a sequence together.

Clear the space: Start by spending a few breaths, or even a few minutes, sitting or standing quietly on your mat. Perhaps close your eyes. Focus on your breath. You can incorporate some simple breathing exercises (examples are given in Chapter 3). Create space between what you've been doing in your day so far and the beginning of your yoga practice.

Make it organic: Your warm up will likely incorporate a number of yoga poses but also incorporate shapes that are not traditional yoga poses. Do what feels good in your body. It knows what it needs: stretch, strengthen, rest, be active. Work according to how you feel and draw in movements that are relevant to your final pose.

Smooth transitions: Consider whether your ultimate pose is a standing posture or a seated posture or one between the two. Think about where you begin your warm up. For example, will you begin supine or seated or standing up? You want to move smoothly from where you begin the sequence to where it will end. Vary your sequences for different poses. Begin some standing, others supine. Explore using different movements even where there are common warm-up areas across poses.

Progressive poses: Ensure your poses are practiced progressively so you don't move into deep poses without adequately preparing the body. View less challenging variations and preparatory poses as an *offering to the temple*.

Counter-poses: If you have moved into some deep poses during your practice, such as backbends, consider whether you need to practice counter-poses even if your body feels as though it doesn't need to. Give your body, which is a temple, the opportunity to benefit from the peak pose as well as time to adjust back into a more neutral position. Each and every *asana is a prayer*.

Close your practice: Aim to end your practice with at least a few moments in a restful pose or even several poses, culminating in Savasana. Savasana is the ultimate prayer and brings an overall sense of relaxation and completeness to your practice.

The sequences you create using the approach in this chapter are likely to be short, perhaps only taking five minutes or so. The idea here is not only to get your home practice started, but also to think about smart and creative sequencing for the temple that is your body.

You might find it useful to record your sequences. You might video the sequence or write it out, enabling you to repeat the practice or even refine it.

Use this approach to build sequences for your favored poses and then go on to explore sequences for less-favored poses. You might surprise yourself and come to enjoy such poses. Aim to build creativity in your sequences as you become more adept. This won't take long. *Asanas are your prayers*.

Example sequences

The following poses illustrate these principles. It is assumed you will have opened the sequence with some moments of stillness to clear the space and will end the sequence with a restful pose. These sequences also focus on just a few aspects/areas to be warmed up in each pose, but you may want to create extended sequences.

Cat cow pose

This pose is often used as a warm-up pose, so the challenge here is to build a warm-up sequence for a warm-up pose. The diagram below shows three areas of the body that can be used to build a sequence.

- The wrists, as they bear some body weight in the movement between cat and cow.

- The shoulders, as they are activated and draw down away from the neck.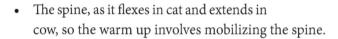

- The spine, as it flexes in cat and extends in cow, so the warm up involves mobilizing the spine.

SEQUENCE

Using these three points, the following is a suggested sequence leading to cat cow pose.

1. Find a comfortable seat (Vajrasana in this example) and let the arms relax by your side. Circle your shoulders forwards and then circle them backwards. Do this three to five times in each direction.

2. Activate your arms by stretching them up into Urdhva Hastasana. Reach up a little further and then hug your shoulder blades down your back. Repeat these two small movements three to five times. Keeping your arms lifted, circle your wrists a few times in each direction. Lower your arms and relax, perhaps circling the shoulders back a few times.

3. Interlace your fingers in front of you and then round the back and stretch the arms forward. From there, straighten the back and lift your arms above your head. Repeat three to five times. This is, essentially, a seated cat cow, mobilizing the spine in a gentle way.

4. Take a small twist to further mobilize the spine, twisting to the right then to the left.

5. Move into an active Balasana, stretching the arms forward, elbows off the mat and tips of the fingers pressing into the mat. Practice drawing the shoulders away from your ears as you would in the final pose.

6. Now move to a table-top position and transition between cat and cow. Repeat three to five times.

You can complete the sequence by resting in Balasana.

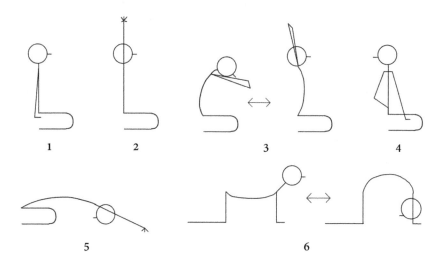

Vrksasana

This is a classic standing and balancing posture. The warm up focuses on external rotation of the upper leg and the balancing aspect of the pose.

The diagram below shows the areas of the body to be warmed up.

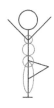

- The legs are to be activated, as the pose involves balancing on one leg.

- The lifted leg will be externally rotated at the hip joint, so the hip needs to be appropriately warmed up with a shape that moves in the same direction.

- The torso needs to be activated and elongated.

- The shoulders need to be mobilized, as the arms will be lifted in the final pose.

SEQUENCE

1. Begin in a supine position with the legs stretched. Point and flex your feet a few times to activate the legs. Then hug the right knee in and move the leg gently from side to side.

2. Now bring the right leg into Ardha Ananda Balasana to deepen the hip opener, and then draw the sole of the left foot onto the floor.

3. From here, place the right foot above the left knee, creating a figure 4 shape, and draw both legs towards you whilst threading the right arm through the legs to hold behind the left leg. This externally rotates the thigh and hip, mirroring the shape of the lifted leg in the final pose. You can also activate your left leg by extending it up to the ceiling.

4. Repeat steps 1–3 on the left side.

5. Find your way to a table-top position.

6. Step your right foot between your hands. Rise up into Anjaneyasana, elongating your spine. To elongate the torso further, stretch to each side, using a yoga brick if your hand does not reach to the floor. Find your way back to table top. Practice the sequence on the left side.

7. Now walk your hands towards your feet so that you come into a crouching position on the balls of your feet. Bring the hands to Anjali mudra and balance. Remaining on the balls of your feet, rise up slowly, retaining the balance if you can.

8. Lower your heels and lower your arms into Tadasana.

9. From Tadasana, move slowly into Vrksasana on each side, exploring different arm positions.

Complete the sequence by standing quietly in Tadasana with your eyes closed and hands in Anjali mudra.

1 2 3

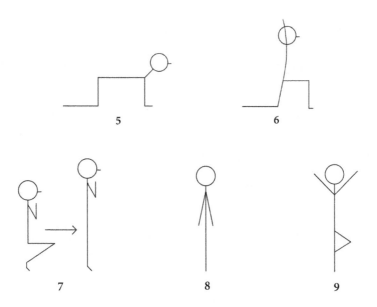

Trikonasana

This is a pose involving the whole body (see the diagram below), so the warm-up sequence aims to heat the body overall, as well as to focus on specific areas for the pose.

- The legs need to be activated, as the front leg is externally rotated and the back leg is internally rotated.

- The hips need to be mobilized in order to create the triangle shape with the legs.

- The torso needs to be elongated and slightly twisted, with the front body facing forwards.

- The shoulders also need to be mobilized, as the arms are extended outwards.

SEQUENCE

1. This sequence aims to heat the body. Standing in Tadasana, raise the arms above the head, and then bend the knees, fold forwards

45 degrees with the spine elongated and take the arms above the back into a skiing stance. From there, raise the arms into Utkatasana and then return to Tadasana. Repeat this three to five times.

2. From Tadasana, take the weight into your right foot, lift the left foot and step it back into a lunge. Hold the lunge for a few breaths whilst activating your back leg and extending your torso.

3. Slowly lower the back knee to the floor and hold Anjaneyasana for a few breaths. This warms the hips.

4. Take the hands to either side of your front foot and slowly extend your front leg, flexing the foot and elongating your torso over the leg (you might want to place your hands on blocks here). Then re-bend the front knee. Repeat this three to five times, gently stretching the hamstrings of your front leg and mobilizing the leg muscles. Re-bend your right knee.

5. Tuck your back toes under. Bring the hands to Anjali mudra in front of your heart and then twist, taking the left elbow over your right leg. Hold for a few breaths before slowly lifting and extending the back leg. This twist mobilizes the spine for the final pose.

6. Release the hands to the floor and walk them around to the left side so that you come into Prasarita Padottanasana. Use blocks for your hands if they do not comfortably reach the floor. Place your right hand on your left leg, extend your torso forwards (it will lift some) and raise your left arm for a further twist and extension of the arms/mobilization of the shoulders as in the final pose. Hold for a few breaths.

7. Release the hands to the floor and move into a low lunge.

8. From the low lunge, ground the back heel and move into Virabhadrasana 2, extending through your fingertips.

9. Straighten your right leg, and stretch the right arm forward along with your torso as you move into Trikonasana. Focus on twisting the front body forwards.

To come out of Trikonasana, move back into Virabhadrasana 2 and then step your left foot forward into Tadasana. Now repeat the sequence from step 2 on the left side. You can close the sequence by spending a few quiet moments in Tadasana.

Adho Mukha Svanasana

This is another pose involving the whole body in the form of a forward fold with the hands, arms and shoulders bearing weight in addition to both feet. This mini sequence focuses on heating the body overall and warming up some key areas for the pose as shown in the diagram below.

- The hamstrings are to be gently warmed and lengthened.

- The lower back is lengthened.

- As the shoulders bear weight in this pose, the shoulders are warmed and strengthened.

SEQUENCE

1. This sequence aims to heat the body. Starting in Tadasana, move into Utkatasana and hold. Aside from being a heating pose, Utkatasana strengthens the back and shoulders. From there, bring the hands to Anjali mudra in front of the heart and twist by bringing the left elbow over the right leg. Hold for a few breaths and then slowly unwind from the twist. As you do so, start to transfer your weight into the right foot and left the left leg into Virabhadrasana 3. Hold the pose for as long as it feels comfortable and then lower the left foot next to the right foot, moving back into Tadasana. Repeat on the left side.

2. In Tadasana, separate the feet to hip distance apart. Roll the spine, leading with the head, into Uttanasana. Have a slight bend in your knees and gently lengthen your hamstrings and lower back. Place your hands on blocks or on the floor.

3. Move into Ardha Uttanasana.

4. Now lower your hands to the mat and walk them forward into plank pose. Hold for a few breaths, strengthening your shoulders, and then lower onto the front of your body.

5. Lift your legs, arms and upper body into Salabhasana. This is a

heating pose that lengthens and strengthens the back. Hold for a few breaths and then relax. Repeat.

6. Move to an all-fours position and move between cat and cow, releasing the back.

7. Now move into Adho Mukha Svanasana. Hold for a few breaths and then come back to an all-fours position. Repeat.

You could end the sequence by resting in Balasana.

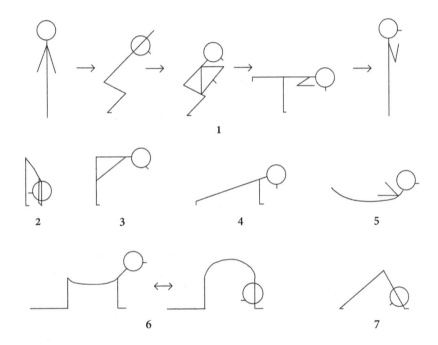

Ardha Dhanurasana

Ardha Dhanurasana is a heating backbending pose. The diagram below shows the areas to be warmed up.

- The thighs need to be warmed and stretched.

- There is a strong upper back focus in this pose, so the warm up opens this area.

- The shoulders also need to be warm and open.

- Overall, the lifting of one leg with the arm on the same side requires strength in the posterior chain muscles.

SEQUENCE

1. Starting from an all-fours position, extend the right leg behind and look forward, creating a gentle backbending shape. Draw your right knee to your nose. Repeat three times and then practice on the left side.

2. From an all-fours position, walk your hands forward into Anahastasana. The aim here is to find a shape that allows your shoulders and upper arms to stretch.

3. Move into Salamba Bhujangasana. Focus on opening the upper back, not the lower back, by gently moving your heart forward.

4. Now find your way into Adho Mukha Svanasana. Hold this pose for a few breaths before moving to plank. Experiment with moving between these two poses, creating heat and strength in your body.

5. From Adho Mukha Svanasana, step your right foot between your hands and move into Anjaneyasana. Hold for a few breaths and focus on the gentle stretch of the left thigh muscles. From here, take your arms into Gomukasana (with the left elbow pointing upwards) and hold for a few breaths. Hold on to a strap if your hands do not meet behind your back. You are continuing to warm the upper back and shoulders. Repeat this step on the left side.

6. Find your way back to Adho Mukha Svanasana. Step your right foot to the outside of your right hand and lower your back knee to the mat. Take your right hand to your lower back and twist to the right. Hold and breathe. Then deepen the pose by lifting your left toes and holding them with your right hand (or you can loop a strap around your left foot). This creates a strong stretch in the

thigh of the back leg. This pose also creates a small backbending shape in the upper back and opens the shoulders. Repeat on the left side.

7. Moving onto your belly, stretch your arms forward, lifting them and your legs into a strong version of Salabhasana. This pose is heating your body and strengthening the posterior chain muscles. Hold for a few breaths and then rest. Repeat.

8. Now you are ready to practice Ardha Dhanurasana on the right and left sides.

You might like to end this sequence by lying on the front of your body, with the backs of your hands supporting your forehead.

Paschimottanasana

This is a seated, forward-folding pose. It is a deeper forward fold than Adho Mukha Svanasana and is one that many people find challenging due to tightness in the hamstrings and/or lower back. The sequence therefore focuses on these areas. The diagram below shows the areas to be warmed up.

- The legs are to be activated.

- The hamstrings are to be gently stretched.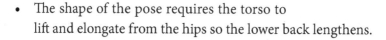

- The shape of the pose requires the torso to lift and elongate from the hips so the lower back lengthens.

SEQUENCE

1. Standing with the feet hip distance apart, place your hands on the sides of your lower ribs. As you breathe in, use your hands to lift and lengthen your torso in an upwards direction. Relax as you breathe out. Repeat a few times, sensing length in your upper body.

2. With your hands on your hips, inhale and lift your right leg with the knee bent and foot flexed (this activates the leg). Then, as you exhale, extend your arms forward at shoulder height and extend your right leg (with the foot still flexed) out in front of you. Place your foot back on the floor, relax your arms and then practice on the left side. Practice a couple of times on each side.

3. Roll down into Uttanasana. Move between Ardha Uttanasana and Uttanasana a few times, softly lengthening your hamstrings. Finish by spending a few breaths in Uttanasana, focusing on lengthening your back.

4. Spend a few breaths in Adho Mukha Svanasana.

5. Step your right foot forward and lengthen your torso. Now lengthen your right leg and flex your right foot, lengthening your hamstrings. Hold for a few breaths and then fold over the right leg to gently deepen the stretch. Switch sides.

6. Find your way onto your back, hug your knees in and then drop

your legs to the right side. Place your right hand on your left knee and stretch your left arm out on the mat in line with your shoulder. Relax and focus on the sensation/stretch in your left side and lower back. Switch sides.

7. Sitting with your legs stretched out and feet flexed, take a belt around your feet and hold the ends in each hand. Use tension in the strap to lift up from the pelvis, creating length from the base of your spine to the crown of your head. The aim here is to be in an upright version of Paschimottanasana, experimenting with gaining length in your hamstrings and back.

8. Now fold forward into Paschimottanasana, maintaining the length you created in your body in step 7.

You might like to complete the sequence by lying on your back, hugging your knees into your chest and rocking from side to side. As you hug your knees, remember: *if your body feels more like a temple then asanas are your prayers.*

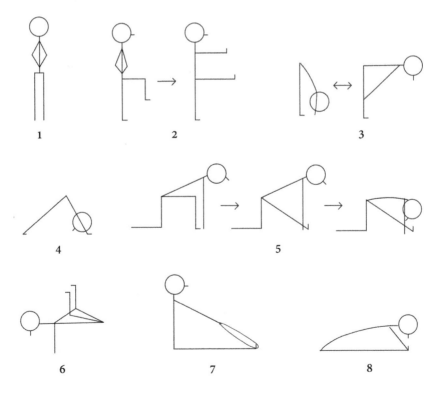

Summary

- Create a foundation for building your home practice by going back to basics. Begin with just your physical practice. Let that be your focus and a way to create presence. Then, as your home practice develops, layer it with breath-work, meditation, intention, meaning and much more.

- Identify a pose that will be the climax of your sequence. It needn't be a pose that might usually be regarded as a peak pose. You could take a warm-up pose or any shape that resonates with you.

- Think about the shape of the pose and key areas of your body that need to be prepared. Draw a diagram so you can see the shape and use it to pinpoint warm-up areas.

- Get on your mat and move through your sequence. Your body is the place where the heart of you dwells; you might regard your body as a temple. As you move through your sequence, keep your body safe and nourish it with practice. *Asana is your prayer.*

— Chapter 3 —

BREATHING LIFE INTO YOU AND YOUR PRACTICE

Breathing in yoga

Breathing is the thread that runs throughout your yoga practice. You literally breathe life into whatever your practice consists of, whether it's movement or meditation, for example. The breath is magical in the way it can calm the nervous system and bring you into the present moment, just as Thich Nhat Hanh describes in his poem "Being Peace": "Breathing in, I calm body and mind. Breathing out, I smile. Dwelling in the present moment I know this is the only moment."

Being in the moment will never disappoint. Try it now. *Breathe in, feel calm, breathe out and smile.*

In yoga, the general aim is to develop a smooth, steady, expansive breath that is audible to you. A fullness of the lungs is achieved as the air is drawn in, expanding the thoracic area in all directions: forwards, sideways, into the backs of the ribs, upwards into the top of the chest and downwards into the belly. Equally, there is a full emptying of the lungs as the air is expelled. This way of breathing should have a natural quality of freedom. A forced, uncomfortable breath defeats the objective. If you practice focusing on your breath right now, even if your breath is not completely steady and expansive, you will still cultivate some sense of freedom. The key is to keep the breath moving and develop a deep connection to it.

Although cultivating a steady and expansive breath should be your focus, you should also allow the breath to guide you. The paradox is that the focus needs to change or soften so that you remain with your breath but you let it be your guide. As your home practice builds, begin by focusing on having a steady and expansive breath. Use the breathing exercises offered in this chapter. Then, as your practice progresses over time, soften that focus so that your breath moves your practice into a more intuitive, energetic realm.

The breath is also an internal barometer of how you are feeling. For example, the breath may be shallow and rapid when anxious, slow when tired or even when feeling balanced. Recognizing the quality of your breath helps with reading your body, which holds much emotion. We often feel emotions in the body or with the breath before the mind has registered that feeling. If you need to, you can use your breath to change a feeling. For example, if you feel anxious, you can explore using an elongated out-breath practice to create a sense of relaxation. The quality of your breath should also be used as a barometer of your experience in a pose. If the breath changes from being full to shallow as you struggle to hold a pose, it's a clear signal to exit from the pose.

Following the breath and maintaining a good quality to the breath is challenging. Perhaps you can achieve that during a seated meditation but lose the thread and quality of breathing when moving. Some students say they find it difficult to know when to breathe in and when to breathe out when flowing through yoga sequences. As a teacher, deep familiarity with breathing practices and your own breath will support your students in their practice. Having a deep connection to your breath will bring a greater sense of presence to the classes you teach. With practice, you will begin to see if your students are breathing well, but first you need to be familiar with your own breath. *Be present by inhaling, calm your body, exhale and smile. With the help of your breath, treat this as the only moment.*

Breathing as a metaphor

Rather than just placing awareness on your breath, it can be helpful to think of both the physical and energetic aspects of the breath as a metaphor for a whole range of things. The physical aspects of breathing can be seen and felt as the body moves: the rib cage and belly expand as the lungs inflate and then they contract when the lungs deflate. The energetic aspects of breathing, as air is drawn in and out, can be visualized. By focusing on these physical and/or energetic concepts, you can compare them to a range of metaphors when you begin your practice or you can weave this idea through your entire practice. It's a way to retain focus on your breath and create presence. The following are some metaphors I have used in my practice:

a. You can think of each in-breath as being expansive, energizing and empowering, with the out-breath being contracting, calming and softening. I use this metaphor on days when I'm feeling tired or just need to slow down. It's a visualization that brings energetic strength balanced with some relaxation.

b. You can imagine the in-breath is a breathing in of something new, perhaps it's an idea, something you are striving for or a vision. You can then imagine the out-breath is a letting go or a clearing of the old, something that needs to change so that you can bring in the new.

c. Experiment with feeling a sense of fullness and satisfaction as you breathe in, with the out-breath creating a sense of contentedly dropping down, rooting, a restorative heaviness.

d. You might like to explore in your mind how the in-breath and the out-breath are a pulsation between opposites of one thing (like a coin has two sides). You cannot have one without the other. The paradox is that they are a whole, and you may wish to use this exercise to embrace elements of paradox in your life.

These metaphors can have a powerful effect. To give an example, a few years ago, after living in central London, I had an extraordinarily strong feeling of wanting to live somewhere very green. I used metaphor (b) to explore this feeling. I would breathe in an image of huge, leafy trees and beautiful rolling countryside and breathe out an image of leaving London. I also used metaphor (d). Although part of me was longing to leave London, the paradox was that I had a strong sense of belonging there. It's where I grew up and had lived all my life, surrounded by family, friends and clients. The thought of leaving all of this was frightening, yet the feeling to leave was overwhelming. I also had no idea where the beautiful green place was. In my breathing practice, I would use these metaphors without any expectation of answers. I would simply dwell in the practice of my breath in the present moment. With time, these feelings and images would translate into a huge shift in my life and it came at a time when I felt ready for and accepting of the change. My husband and I left London and moved to the incredibly beautiful mountains of North Carolina.

This practice of using the breath as a metaphor also links with practices of stillness and listening, which are explored in the next chapter. These practices are illuminating, both on and off the mat, and I would encourage you to explore them.

Breath exercises

As an experienced yoga practitioner, you will be familiar with a range of traditional breathing techniques, but this section takes breath-work back to basics. There is a beauty to working with simple techniques. Aside from helping to develop a steady, expansive and more consistent breath practice, you'll likely find they are simple to practice. They can become a part of who you are rather than something you just do. They add a richness to the experience of the practice.

When working with the breath, notice where there is movement in your body or whether anything comes up for you. When I breathe, I'm aware I have a tendency to breathe more into the top of my chest, but on days when I feel anxious, I feel a restriction of my breath in this area. My breathing might feel jagged too. I use these sensations to select a breath practice that will be calming and make me smile. I aim to remain tuned to how I feel during the exercise and once I've completed it.

Below are the breath exercises I use most often in my home practice.

Shoulder shrugs

1. As you inhale, shrug your shoulders up to your ears.

2. Continue to hold your shoulders up as you exhale and inhale again, focusing entirely on your breath.

3. As you exhale, circle your shoulders back and down.

Note whether you connect more deeply to the exhale when you release your shoulders. Was it possible to breathe expansively with the shoulders shrugged?

Rib-cage expansion

1. Place the four fingers of each hand on your lower front ribs with the thumbs resting on the backs of the ribs.

2. Feel your thumbs.

3. As you inhale, sense the expansion of the rib cage forwards, sideways and backwards into your hands.

4. As you exhale, follow the shrinking movement of the rib cage with your hands.

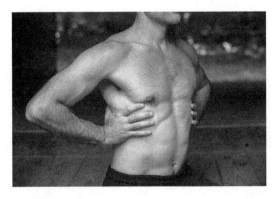

Note whether this exercise brings you deeper into your body. I have to focus on not flaring my front ribs and on expanding into the back of the ribs.

Exhale focus

1. Take a full breath in.

2. Exhale.

3. Then exhale a little more so that your lungs are completely empty of air.

Note whether there's a deeper softening in your body on the exhale. Note whether the in-breath comes more naturally after a fuller exhale.

Heart-centered breathing

1. Be seated with your left hand resting on the left side of your chest around the space of your heart. Place your right hand on top of the left and then lighten the placement of your hands slightly.

2. As you inhale, imagine you are drawing energy into your heart space.

3. As you exhale, imagine you are radiating energy from your heart around your body.

4. Practice this for a few more breaths, being aware of the movement of your chest and hands.

How does this breathing exercise make you feel? Do you feel more drawn into yourself or your heart center?

Belly breathing

1. Lay down on your mat and place both hands on your lower belly.

2. As you inhale, draw your breath down to your belly and feel your belly rise.

3. As you exhale, notice how the belly falls.

4. As you continue to breathe, register information from your fingertips regarding the quality of your breathing.

How does this make you feel? For me, drawing the breath down to my belly requires a hint of extra effort, but the effort is rewarded with a deeper sense of relaxation on the exhale. The physical connection of the hands to my breath creates a greater feeling of presence.

As with the breathing metaphors, these breath exercises can be much more than a mat practice. Their broader application in daily life can be a powerful tool for creating moment-by moment presence. For example, during the COVID-19 pandemic, I often felt disconnected from family, friends and so much more. I used the heart-centered practice on almost daily basis to find a sense of grounding. I also felt much sadness for the loss of so much during this period. Focusing on my exhale allowed me to fold into that feeling and be present with it, rather than push it away. After a couple of minutes of the exhale focus, the sadness would pass. I'd feel calm and was able to smile.

Spend time in your practice experimenting with breath-awareness exercises. Find the ones that work for you and use these practices to support you in your daily life.

Linking breath with movement

In all probability, you will have trained or are training in a tradition that links breath and movement, and that's how you teach. The link between breath and movement is likely to be very intuitive for you but having that focus on a consistent basis in your practice is not always easy to achieve. The mind wanders. The skill is to refocus and find ways to maintain the breath focus. You could, for example, infuse your practice with slow, mindful movements, with the in- and out-breaths elongated to match the movement. Use the breath to feel and delve into the poses so there's a highly interactive experience between breath and body. Creating this kind of awareness in your practice will also greatly enhance your ability to describe and cue poses in your teaching.

Use the breath to inform a pose

Being connected to your breath can truly inform your experience in a pose. Use the breath to notice how your body moves in a pose, even if those movements are subtle. Also notice how the shape of a pose deepens or feels more accessible as you breathe into its shape. In your home practice, commit to this very simple practice of using the breath to inform a pose. It will enrich your practice and make you smile.

The mind, body and breath are in a constant state of movement and change; regard the experience of practicing asana in the same way. Let there be a constant process of evaluation, learning and relearning. Use the breath to support this process, perhaps even reorganize yourself in poses to change your perspective. Below is an example of how I recently explored Vrksasana in this way.

1. **Inhale:** As I prepare to move into the posture, I use the inhale to slowly slide my foot up the inner seam of my leg before reaching my hand to place the foot inside of my leg. I'm aware of the sense of touch of my toes on my opposite leg.

2. **Exhale:** I softly bring my hands to Anjali mudra in front of my heart. I feel a little stiffness in the hip of the lifted leg as I seek to draw the knee out to the side and some clicking in the joint. I wobble. I move slowly into external rotation of the hip but only take the shape part of the way.

3. **Inhale:** I anchor the standing foot into the ground and draw up through my torso. I feel more balanced with the inhale.

4. **Exhale:** My body softens, easing into the pose. I acknowledge that I cannot move the knee fully out to the side today so settle into the modified shape.

5. **Inhale:** I draw the breath up through the crown of my head and feel my shoulders retract.

6. **Exhale:** I softly step my lifted foot back to the ground.

I used the breath to inspire a sense of grace whilst moving in and out of the posture. I noticed subtle movements of grounding, lengthening, expansion and softening whilst in the pose. The sensation in my hip also helped maintain presence to the practice. I didn't struggle to move into more of a classic shape but accepted the shape in its more comfortable, modified form. I reorganized myself into a shape that is different from the way I often practice the pose. With a home practice, you can take your time to explore and refine the way you practice.

Explore individual poses in this way. Use the breath to learn about your experience in poses. Explore with your breath what you are experiencing, what might be changing and, perhaps, what needs to change.

Use the breath to inspire sequences

Stand in Tadasana and take a few very focused, slow, deep breaths. Observe whether your body feels like moving in an intuitive way with those breaths. For example, it might feel very natural to raise your arms on the inhale and lower them on the exhale. Or you might want to lift one arm on the inhale and stretch sideways on the exhale. If you tune fully into each breath, it is likely this will inspire you to move. Use the breath to explore creative movement so that you move differently each time you practice, creating interest and variety in your practice.

As an exercise, take an individual pose and allow your breath to sequence you into the pose (without any prior planning). Your breath is likely to infuse your practice with different shapes and creative, neat transitions between poses. Below is an example of how the breath inspired a short sequence to Ardha Dhanurasana in my practice.

1. I begin by lying on the front of my body, with my forehead resting on the backs of my hands.

2. **Inhale:** I lift and extend my right leg to lengthen it. I sense extension along my entire leg all the way to the tips of my toes.

3. **Exhale:** I lower the leg whilst maintaining the extension created. Energetically, the right leg feels longer than the left leg. In fact,

there's a feeling of greater length along the entire right side of my body.

4. I repeat steps 2–3 on the left side and now my legs feel an equal length.

5. **Inhale**: I rise into Salamba Bhujangasana.

6. **Exhale**: Intuitively, I press my forearms a little more into the mat. This pose feels open, so I lift the heart space a fraction more. I continue to explore Salamba Bhujangasana pose for a few more breaths, moving the head to look right and then left.

7. **Inhale**: I bend my right knee.

8. **Exhale**: I reach back with my right hand to hold the right foot. I find the foot easily, but I notice my right shoulder feels a little stiff.

9. **Inhale**: I softly move my right foot back and feel the connection between my right foot and shoulder.

10. **Exhale**: I then lift my left arm off the mat into a fuller expression of Ardha Dhanurasana. I remain in the pose for a few breaths. I notice how my body heats and how my breath becomes a little labored so I then release out of the pose and move to the left side.

Experiment with this idea of using your breath to create peak-pose sequences. Allow your breath to take you through a process of discovery. You may well find that, after you've practiced the peak pose, you'll continue your practice in a way that is inspired by your breath.

Another approach is not to have a peak pose in mind but to get on your mat and start to move with your breath as if it were the only moment. Try it and see where that movement takes you. This way of practicing features regularly in my own practice. You essentially begin your practice with a blank canvas, but it is the breath that paints the picture of your practice. You'll be in the present moment.

Summary

- Spend time cultivating smooth, steady, expansive breathing. Carve out a few minutes each day to do this.

- The breath is a transformative tool to use in your daily life. Identify the breath-awareness exercises that resonate with you and use them on and off your mat.

- Can you use the breath as a barometer of how you are feeling? Equally, can you use the breath to influence the way you are feeling?

- Breathing can fully inform the shapes you create.

- Allow the breath to inspire movement in your practice. The breath might lead you into traditional yoga shapes or it might lead you into some movements not typically associated with yoga. Just let the breath be a guide in your practice.

Chapter 4

ENGAGE WITH THE EXPERIENCE OF YOUR YOGA PRACTICE

The importance of "hearing"

We are human beings, but you may have heard the expression that we are human doings. We can be in a state of acceleration, living life on autopilot, juggling a career with family life and making ends meet, such that we become disconnected from our feelings. We don't always find time to feel, listen and truly experience the present moment. We are so often in our thinking minds rather than in our bodies. The same can be true of a yoga practice. Yoga is an experience which means that, although it is something you do, it also requires observation. Yoga needs to be practiced in a connected way so you can hear your practice through feeling and sensing it. As Ram Dass said in *Be Here Now*: "The quieter you become, the more you can hear."

Once you recognize the full experience of your practice, you will be cloaking it in a quality of authenticity. Your students will recognize and value your authenticity and that will bring an infinite richness to your teaching.

So, how do you hear or feel your practice? On the one hand, you need some discipline around getting on your mat, but you also need to approach that discipline with harmony and balance. That in itself requires awareness of what you are feeling and how and why you are practicing. You need to find the spark within you to practice, such that you are touched by your practice and can find an inner joy to it. You then nurture these feelings. Explore silence and stillness in a way that resonates with you because *the quieter you become, the more you can hear*. That could be through meditation, breath-work, restorative poses, yin yoga and Savasana, for example. The key is to practice observation and reflection to be with the experience that truly sits within the cave of your heart.

Move from your thinking self to your feeling self

The spark within you

Begin by asking what makes you want to have a home yoga practice or why you already have an established home practice. What is the spark within you that makes you want to practice? What does the spark feel like or look like? Can you easily recognize and describe it? Is it helpful to sit with the question in your meditation practice and see what arises? Knowing your spark will make the practice of yoga part of who you are, such that you'll want to return to your practice time and time again.

For me, the spark feels like a playful, energetic flow from me. It's about my love of creative movement and experiencing the magic of my breath, as well as it being a spiritual experience that constantly unfolds. It gives me a feeling of being fully alive and a sense that we are all greater than the sum of our parts. Your spark might have some of the same, but it will be different, for sure. For you, it might be about ritual, something magical, therapeutics, biomechanics, alignment, meditation, philosophy to list a few. Explore and know your spark.

You might also want to ask a similar question each time you come to practice: "Why am I practicing yoga today?" Listen to your answer to see if it has the spark. Responses such as, "I need to improve my practice" or "I have classes to plan" may be totally valid but they lack feeling and sparkle. They don't give a sense of something you might want to nurture. These are "thinking" responses; they are more in your head than your heart. There's certainly a place for these thinking responses. The next chapter explores using some thinking responses, such as looking at your mindset and knowledge, alongside feeling responses to deepen your practice.

Instead, recognize a feeling you hope to create and see if that brings you closer to the spark. For example, you might respond, "I know I'm going to feel great after the practice" or "I love the feeling of lightness in my body after I've moved, meditated and breathed." Equally, you might say, "I always feel tired and short of time. There's a chance I will feel more fatigued at the end of the practice, but I'll be glad I made the effort." These feeling responses give a more personal, authentic layer to the meaning of your practice. There's personal awareness in the responses and a spark. This is true even if the response is not a wholly positive one, as in the last example. The hearing is to acknowledge the feeling, whatever it may be, and be receptive to it.

Feeling to hear each practice

Be curious about how you are feeling as you practice. Feelings need a pathway, an outlet. Observe them and tune in to what you are sensing. Listen to what is there and not what you hope to find. It's a powerful way to bring presence to your practice.

Ask yourself the following questions.

- How do I feel as I decide to practice and get on my mat?

- How do I feel during the practice? Does it change throughout the practice?

- How do I feel at the end of my practice?

By way of an example, this is what I observed in a recent practice: I arrived on my mat overflowing with irritation after a disagreement with a friend. I hoped to feel a sense of release and a calmer state of mind after the practice. I practiced focusing on the pause between each inhale and exhale. This helped me feel more centered but I still felt irked. I listened. I felt the need to move in a way that might release some of the emotion, so I flowed through a dynamic practice. As I moved, I gradually found a feeling of freedom from having voiced my opinion in the argument.

It was the right thing to do. At the end of the practice, when I was in Savasana, I felt tired, less bothered by the argument, sorry I'd upset my friend and some satisfaction having spoken my truth. I practiced in a way that was connected to my feelings. I listened to them. To some extent, they directed my practice but my practice also changed the way I felt. *The quieter you become, the more you can hear.*

This is an example where emotions were strong and easier to stay connected to. It can take effort to stay tuned to the experience of a practice when feelings are more even keeled or on a day that is typical for you. Noticing when your mind wanders is the challenge, but when you do so you can recommit to the experience.

Always practice with curiosity. Tune in to what are you sensing. Sensation is information. Perhaps you feel vitality, strength and courage on one day and then restlessness and boredom on the next. On another, you might feel balanced and content or anxious and fearful. Notice these sensations in order to navigate inwards. This level of observation may require some discipline but it will become second nature with time, if it hasn't already become part of your practice. It's all part of the hearing.

The power of intention

Having an intention creates an anchor for your practice. It's the keystone from which your experience can build and deepen. It's not essential to practice with an intention, and the pure act of just getting on your mat and practicing is amazing, but practicing with an intention is a way to hear and connect to your inner self.

Intention setting

Notice how and when you set an intention and whether you often practice with one. Does setting an intention come easily to you. Do you like to sit with your thoughts, perhaps in meditation, to be able to set one? Sometimes, identifying an intention requires deep thought but setting an intention can also be felt in your body. Be aware of your processes for setting an intention, noticing if you become distracted. This is all part of the experience. If it's difficult to set an intention, explore within yourself why that is. Be honest about it. The mind has a crafty way to deflect issues, which might be a very worthy topic for an intention. The appropriate intention is within you; *if you become quiet enough, you will hear it.*

An intention should be meaningful to you but should also give meaning to your practice. Consider the quality of your intention. Is it clear, a little muddled or incomplete? Each of these, or anything in between, is your experience. Connect to what is going on in your mind, body and breath as you set an intention. Be fully aware of what your experience is.

Below are some ideas on how to set an intention. Most involve gathering issues in your life and bringing them into your practice on the mat because that is, in essence, the yoga practice.

You might ask if there's anything you need in your life right now. In my own practice, for example, I've explored creating more time and space for myself, creating stability when things have felt off-track, feeling stronger when I've been sick and finding a way to manage a difficult situation.

You can ask if there's anything you are hoping to achieve. Crafting a vision for my career has featured regularly in my intention setting over the years. I've then taken bite-sized pieces of that vision or longer-term goal so that it has a current context and is practiced with presence. For example, I've had a goal of writing and publishing this book, but in my practice, I've been working with the intention of finding creative and interesting content for each chapter. I slowed my practice down in order to quieten my mind. I found that ideas then came to me.

Mindfulness experts recommend practicing with gratitude. You can use your practice to be thankful for many things: your life, the ground you walk on, your home, cherished friends and loved ones, for example.

Reading and listening to podcasts can be an incredible source of inspiration. You might be inspired by a quote and frame an intention around that. For example, a while ago I saw this quote from Lao Tuz: "Nature does not hurry, yet everything is accomplished." That inspired an intention to spend more time in nature, walking, planting and following ecologically sound practices.

Is there a single word or even a short phrase that resonates with you?

The meaning of words is deeply personal and you might want to set an intention based on a word. Take the word "song," for example. As part of a meditation, you could reflect on that word and explore whether an intention comes to mind. When I did this, I knew it was easy for me to listen to music but I also recognized that I sometimes forget to listen to my own song and find the harmonies within. Finding the song within became my intention.

I also draw inspiration from my surroundings. If I come to my mat without an idea for an intention, I can look out of the window and set an intention inspired by what I see. One beautiful spring day I saw a pair of birds cheerily engaged in the gathering of materials for a nest. Inspired by this scene, I set an intention to draw on the earth's energy and to practice with a sense of renewal and abundance.

Draw on your internal and external resources to set an intention. Set it thoughtfully, and with spontaneity if you can, and explore your intention with a loving, open heart.

Linking the intention to your practice

In a home practice, not only can you spend the time you need setting your intention, but you can also make it very relevant to your practice. Tap into your intuition and creativity as you get on the mat to see how your practice can be a reflection of your intention.

What comes up for you when you think of your intention? Using a gratitude practice as an example, explore how gratitude feels or what it looks like. That could be heart-felt and full. You might visualize postures that extend the heart upwards or place your hands on the heart space or in Anjali mudra. Incorporate symbols that resonate in the poses you practice to connect more deeply with your intention.

Are there certain types of movement that resonate with your intention? With my intention to have interesting and creative content for this chapter, I have felt and visualized a feeling of fluidity, trees swaying, a river flowing. These translated into wave-like, rippling movements with my spine, exploring extension and flexion in a number of poses. Another way of looking at this is working with the element of water or any other element that resonates with your intention.

You can work energetically with your intention, or even take it a step further and work with an archetype that represents your intention. For example, if you are seeking a major change in your life, you might want to practice with some fire in your belly or in a dynamic way. An archetype aligned with this type of intention is the Hindu goddess Durga, who is associated with transformation. You can call in the qualities of this goddess, play tunes about Durga and practice poses that are often associated with her qualities, such as courage and strength. If you are working with a softer intention, then, energetically, you might want to move slowly and indulge your body with the breath more so than usual. Or your practice could be one of stillness and/or meditation so that you can fully feel and hear your breath.

These are just a few examples of how intention and practice can be aligned. Tap into your intuition to find the connection.

Maintaining your intention

Our minds are like a motor that is constantly running, so it's no surprise that being fully in the present and hearing and being with the experience of your yoga practice can feel ambitious. You begin with an intention and then it slips your mind for the majority of the practice. Despite this, the fact you've set an intention means you are already tuning into your internal experience. You should savor these moments of absolute presence.

Linking intention to the way you practice, by incorporating movements or symbols as described above, is a way to maintain that connection. The use of consistent shapes can be a potent reminder of your intention. For example, when I practiced while inspired by the quote "Nature does not hurry, yet everything is accomplished," I used Vrksasana throughout my practice in a number of different forms.

The use of a mudra, often a hand gesture but also an expression of other parts of the body, will support your intention in an energetic, symbolic way. There are many recognized mudras within the yoga tradition, but you can use any gesture that epitomizes your intention. For example, when practicing with the intention of renewal and abundance, the mudra I used was a vibrant lifting of my arms above my head with the palms open and fingers spread, as if in a gesture of luminosity. That was my feeling and experience of renewal and abundance.

If you like to sing, use mantra in your practice. If singing is not for you, recite a mantra in your mind or simply speak it. As with mudras, you can create your own mantras or use traditional Sanskrit ones. Find simplicity in your mantra. It could be, "May I have courage" or "I am blessed to have this body." Let the words be a reflection of your intention. You can also write out your intention and have stickies, notes or your journal close by so you have a clear visual of it. Use whatever means you can to embody your intention, making your practice part of who you are. The intention needs to be something you can feel in your body. Ultimately, it is not something you arrive at with your thinking mind but it is something you are feeling. If you are quiet enough, you will feel and hear your intention.

A final word on Savasana

When you've moved through your yoga practice and come into Savasana, have you ever had any light-bulb moments? Have you ever had the experience of something finally making sense, or did you have an amazing idea without putting any effort into the thought of it?

In corpse pose, as you settle into a place between wakefulness and deep rest, you are very much alive. It's a place of living, being and doing nothing. It's a place where the unconscious can become conscious, where pearls of wisdom reveal themselves. It's a place of deep hearing without having to listen because the spirit that dwells in your heart knows it. Make time for Savasana at the closing of your practice. You may find that something relevant to your intention falls into place.

Moving from the global picture to the detail

This chapter has looked at hearing the bigger picture of your yoga experience with emphasis on feeling and sensation. The next chapter moves to hearing within the container of the physical practice itself, with a little more emphasis on the thinking. It moves from the global picture to the detail. Ultimately, there should be a blending of the bigger picture and smaller picture, as well as the feeling and thinking senses, in order to hear completely.

Summary

- Use your yoga practice to totally tune in to your whole being. Use the time on your mat as a contemplative practice and then take that skill out into your wider life.

- Be curious and honest about what you feel as you practice. This brings qualities of presence and authenticity to your practice.

- Find your spark to practice. Sense, feel and listen to know your spark.

- Give meaning to your practice through the power of intention. Let your practice be an affirmation of your intention such that your intention and practice become one.

- Being with the experience, on and off the mat, will bring a heightened awareness to your life. Listen to your heart, but know when to follow your head.

- Make time in the stillness of Savasana to hear.

Chapter 5

YOUR BODY KNOWS

Knowing your limits: practicing with your body and your mind

Yoga is for every type of body and, the chances are, you know your body well. For example, you'll know if you are flexible, hypermobile or injured. You might say your body is inflexible and tight, or perhaps you have a condition that affects your practice or you have the odd nagging ache or pain. It's possible that over the years you have noticed how your body has changed and it now takes longer to recover from strong movement or you can't move so deeply into poses. You may describe your body as having a combination of these things and others. This is knowing your body. Let's call it "knowing your body type." Not only do you know your body, but the paradox is that your body also knows. As a yoga practitioner, the skill is to take what you already know but also accept that there's a wealth of information held within your body. You've got to listen for it and be aware that limitations may not just be physical. They may be emotional, residing in your attitudes and perspectives on life. As Albert Einstein is thought to have said: "Once we know our limits, we go beyond them."

Once you've listened to your body and can recognize your limitations, embrace the messages with all of your heart. *When you truly know your own body and understand your limits, you'll be able to move beyond them.*

How to know what your body knows

At one level, recognizing what your body knows is simple. Much of what it tells you is obvious, for example, you may know your shoulders are tight or you have some pain. Pain is a gift. Your body is speaking directly to you and asking for changes. You'll also have learned plenty in the classroom so you might know what injury to expect if you attempt a deep pose that you are not ready for. Yet, by going a step beyond, there is an opportunity for deep learning from within your own body, because your body knows. It has the capacity to tell you what is better for you and what it needs.

No doubt there will have been occasions in your life when you've been able to rely on a message coming from your body. It might have been an instinct, a feeling or something you just knew. The same can be true in your yoga practice. You've already made the best possible start to connect to and hear what your body knows by practicing yoga. You may already have felt or sensed its transformational effects. You can go further by being fully awake to your practice and your life, feeling, sensing and listening with your whole being. This is being present. *If you love someone, the greatest gift you can give them is your presence. It is also a gift to yourself.*

As you breathe, meditate and move, practice with an infinite humility. Practicing with humility is a mindset. It is also a feeling, which comes from within and then radiates out into the movements you create. Humility means having a deep reverence for your body, and practicing with compassion and gratitude for the way you are physically and emotionally put together. It'll help you to recognize your limits. Regard the movement you create as a privilege. Work with challenge in your practice when it feels right to do so. This way, you can keep your practice safe and moving forward. Turn towards the dark spaces in your practice, perhaps that's something you don't enjoy or things that don't come easily, and surrender to the exploration. Be open minded. Go with your intuition and trust it to connect to your body's wisdom and intelligence.

When you listen for messages from your body, there's also paradox, which is not to listen too hard. It's something that can't be forced.

Sometimes it may even be necessary to let go of the listening because that's when the messages can be heard. They can come in the spaces when the accelerated, thinking mind is calmed.

To give a simple example, my flexible hamstrings made moving into forward folds satisfyingly easy. It was the comfort zone of my practice. When I was on a yoga retreat in a beautiful Mediterranean location, away from the pressures of my day job, I had the warm climate aiding my flexibility. With a quietened mind, each time I moved deeply into forward folds without any discomfort, the feeling of length in my hamstrings instinctively felt wrong. I felt this even though the teacher was praising my flexibility. My body's internal compass of what was appropriate or not was speaking to me. I'd almost let go of the listening, but I heard from my body that I needed to change my practice. I worked on strengthening my hamstrings, which created more support in my pelvis and hips.

This was a habitual pattern that felt great but actually was not. I had to place trust in what I was hearing and feeling and then I had to change my attitude.

Attitude

Attitude, which is often a function of your disposition, is a huge topic and it is only possible to touch on it here. You might say yoga is about having a particular mindset, or you might feel that yoga has affected your attitude or even changed it. In the space of a home practice, you can expand your practice by exploring your attitudes towards how and what you like to practice and also what you do not like to practice and why. Your limits are not just physical; they dwell in the mind too.

Inquire whether your sentiments on the mat are a reflection of your attitudes or even your disposition in day-to-day life. Often, a practice on the mat is a microcosm of life as a whole. As you delve into your attitudes, through thought and feeling, explore tuning into what your body knows and listen for the messages.

As you explore, consider whether you'd like to refine or change any of your attitudes on the mat. For example, if you feel that you want to create more happiness and view life more positively, try singing mantras in your practice on a consistent basis. If you are persistent in this practice, it could help. Similarly, if you are someone who completes 90 percent of projects and then moves on to the next project before finishing, always ensure you complete your yoga practice. Don't skip Savasana. Be consistent in your practice if there are attitudes you'd like to change.

In my practice, forward folds were my go-to comfort place. I had an attitude that yoga was about being flexible. This is where I perceived "success" compared with other posture groups, which felt hindered by my stiff shoulders and a tight back. I also used to practice in a strong, rigid way. My practice was a mirror of a demanding career at that time; being in a constant state of striving, pushing and successful delivery of goals. There wasn't anything wrong with that lifestyle; at times it was very fulfilling. However, with careful listening to my body, I realized I needed more ease and enjoyment. I changed my attitude and practice. There was more softness, fewer forward folds and I focused more on the "stuck" areas of my practice. Yoga was not about being super-flexible. With time and the change of attitude, I found that the stiffer areas of my body opened and became more accessible.

Spend time thinking about the nature of your practice. What type of yoga do you practice: is it strongly dynamic, a soft flow, yin or restorative, or do you mix it up? Is this a reflection of your lifestyle or a response to it?

Then look at the content of your practice: do you practice a broad range of poses or do you favor a particular group of poses? Do you have go-to poses and why is that? Are you able to balance your practice with strength and stretching or do you favor one over the other? Reflect on these questions in relation to your body type. By way of example, I had a newly qualified yoga teacher as a client. Her lower back was especially flexible and much of her home practice consisted of deep, advanced back extensions, which she loved. She came to realize that her practice needed to be balanced out, to some extent, by strengthening and stabilizing her posterior chain muscles and abdominals. As these muscles strengthened, her back-extension practice actually improved. *She found her limits in order to move beyond them.*

Embrace to move beyond your limits

When your body shares its wisdom, accept it and embrace it. Hug your arms around what you hear and then take action. It's the taking of action that enables you to move beyond your limits. Recruit whatever resources you need to take action. Experiment, feel, sense, research, think, use logic, consult with others. Keep your awareness open to learning, hearing and understanding your limits.

In my home practice, I embraced what I heard by exploring different ways to strengthen the muscles that provide a stabilizing action in forward folds. I also allowed my practice to soften. Other posture groups became more accessible and, ironically, my body became more flexible yet integrated and stable. As a result of finding the right balance between strength, stabilization and softness, my physical practice progressed in a safe, enjoyable and rewarding way. Not only that, but my desire to practice mindfulness and to be more present changed. I felt I was becoming more aware and more open. I was moving beyond my limits in both a physical and emotional way.

Engaging with the wisdom of your body, and adapting accordingly, is a continuous and evolving journey. It's a journey you are already on and one that will continue to deepen if you are present to it. Within the space of your home yoga practice, go further on that journey by devotedly exploring individual poses, delve into the detail and listen for the knowing of your body, in order to move beyond your limits.

Knowing is in the detail

In your practice, connect deeply to a pose by taking your time to dwell on its shape and, more importantly, your experience in it. It's a gateway to hearing what your body knows. Submit to the detail of the pose by taking what you know about its alignment, and then fine tune by going on a journey of feeling, sensing and thought. The following section offers some modes of inquiry to *find your limits so you can move beyond them.*

The meaning of a pose to you

When you begin, spend a moment connecting to the essence of the pose, what it means to you, and use that as an anchor for exploration. Just take a few seconds to see what arises: a gut feel, an image, a quality.

By way of example, when I think of Virabhadrasana 2, I feel courage and strength, which are qualities you can use to practice with. For Ustrasana, I see sun radiating upwards from the heart space, this being a helpful image for alignment in the pose. It may be that your image is quite literal yet it can be inspiring. For example, Bhujangasana produces an image of a powerful, yet elegant, unfurling of a cobra's head, which is full of strength and pride. This is a stirring image to use when moving into the pose.

Practicing with what you see as the essence of a pose brings a special, personal quality to your exploration of it. If you can feel the essence of the pose, you are embodying it. Your body will know.

Sensation in the pose

Ask yourself where, in the body, you have the most sensation in the pose. What is that sensation and does it differ from one side to the other? Be incredibly curious. Regard the sensation as a gift of treasure and surrender to it. If you fully participate in the sensation, you are attuned to information from your body.

Take Trikonasana as an example, a pose that may represent harmony to you. Ask yourself whether the shape feels harmonious in your body and then try this: as you move into Trikonasana, press into the mound of your front big toe. Do you feel pressure on the front knee, stuck in the hip of the back leg or too much gravity drawing your torso to the floor? Be aware of the sensations you are experiencing in the pose. Make adjustments if you need to. Now, do you feel all four corners of your feet, do your legs feel strong and is your back elongated and bright with an illumination from your heart as it twists towards the sky? Digest what you feel and explore whether anything further needs to change.

Notice when and where there is movement of your breath and redirect the breath if you need to. For example, in a closed pose such as

Balasana, you may want to direct the breath more into the back body. Also notice if you stop breathing for a moment and whether that can actually be helpful. For example, explore what happens as you transition into a balancing pose such as Vrksasana. Does the breath remain smooth and regular or do you instinctively hold your breath as a way to find balance in the pose? Or perhaps you need to free the breath in some poses. For example, in Setu Bandha Sarvangasana, you might need to move the chin a fraction away from the top of your chest to create a freer flow of breath.

Does your body call for a counter-movement because your body knows, or does it simply want to rest in stillness for a few breaths? Listen for the feedback.

Your attitude in a pose is also sensation. For example, when I practice Ardha Dhanurasana, I can get frustrated with the effort it takes. If I then tune in to sensations in my physical body, I can feel that a narrow line of muscles in my back are strongly activated but probably need to be stronger. That's where the frustration is coming from. My body knows.

Energetics

Dwell on the energetic aspects of the pose. Where do you feel the energy in a pose, where is it drawing from and in which direction do you feel it is going? Consider whether you need to redirect the energy.

There is almost always a polarity of energy in yoga poses. Many poses have a descending energy for stabilization and an ascending energy to enliven the pose. Or you may feel there is an energy that radiates from your core out into the limbs of the body.

By way of illustration, try the following in Trikonasana.

1. Feel that there is a dropping of energy from the pelvis, down the legs to the feet. Through the feet, feel a strong rooting, which, at the same time, gives a sense of activation to lengthen your spine.

2. Equally, find an upward expansion of energy from the pelvis through to the crown of the head.

The breath plays a big part in energetics, and you might like to use visualizations of the breath moving or redirecting energy in your body. As you will know, the inhalation is often associated with a rising, engaging, expanding energy whilst the exhale can direct energy to the source or foundation of a pose and also bring a softening. This can be helpful if the energetics of a pose are disoriented by your feelings from day-to-day life that accompany you onto the mat. For example, if you are rushing and haven't been able to create space between your day and your practice, a descending energetics focus maybe very grounding. You could use this by prolonging the exhalation in standing postures, with a visualization of an anchoring energy through the pelvis, legs and feet. As you arrive on your mat, you might like to set an intention to explore the link between your breath and the energetics of your practice.

Another energetic sensation you can practice is a gathering in of energy together with the polarity of expansion. So there's a containment, which is stabilizing, but also a radiating energy.

Move into Anjaneyasana and try this.

1. Draw the front foot towards the back knee and integrate the front ribs with the back ribs. This is the gathering in of energy.

2. Now illuminate and expand your torso up through to the fingertips.

Play with these energetic polarities and explore how this feels in your body.

Do it differently

Creativity unwraps conditioning. Explore a pose in a way that is not typical for you, not only to create interest in your practice but also to depart from habitual patterns. Exploring the shapes of poses and finding creativity in your practice is explored further in Chapter 7. For example, Paschimottanasana is often practiced in a cooling way, folding forward over the legs. For a change, it could be practiced in a more active way, with a small hinge from the hips (as if you are halfway between Dandasana and Paschimottanasana), aiming to find the sensation of a backbend in your upper back (you might find it helpful to use a strap around your feet to find this sensation). If you are rounded in your spine, you will like this and find it effective. In your practice, explore differences between variations of poses and see what you discover. Listen, because your body knows.

Also be open to the possibility that things which feel odd might actually be beneficial. For example, Salamba Sirsasana should be practiced with the legs in an upright position, but sometimes the legs are slightly to one side. The adjustment to bring the legs to a totally upright position can feel strange, but it is beneficial to bring symmetry to the pose.

Be open to different possibilities. That attitude, in itself, will help you to know your limits and move beyond them.

Alignment

It goes without saying that good alignment in your practice is essential on so many levels. You need to keep your own practice safe and injury free. You need to demonstrate strong alignment to your students and you certainly need to be able to articulate it well. This chapter has not focused on alignment, because you already know this, but be sure to examine the physical aspects of individual poses in your home practice. Take two alignment points, such as the foundation, your feet, legs, spine, shoulders or arms, and focus on these. Be sure to recognize robust, safe alignment in your own practice. Listen for what your body knows.

Through self-enquiry, draw on these varied ways to delve into the detail of your yoga practice and explore what your body knows. It will bring a richness to your practice. *Knowing the details is a way to understand your limits and move beyond them.*

Summary

- Know your body and, in the context of that, recognize how you like and do not like to practice.

- Taking what you know, accept there's more to know, because your body knows. It has an innate wisdom. Listen softly for its intelligence.

- Surrender to, and absorb, the sensations in your practice. Sensation comes in so many forms: sensory messages from the physical and subtle body, feelings, thoughts, your breath. Witness them all; it's your body that's speaking to you.

- Know your ways to know your body by listening in. When you listen, you will know your limits. From there, embrace those limits and carefully find ways to move beyond them. It's not necessarily about movement. Expand your consciousness, which has limitless potential. This is the larger practice of yoga.

Chapter 6

CREATING MEANING FROM THE SHAPES YOU CREATE

New perspectives in your practice

Through the power of intention, aim to create new perspectives in your practice. As John O'Donohue said in *Anam Cara*: "The way you look at things is the most powerful force in shaping your life."

In this chapter, we set an intention in a way that can be fully felt in your body when you practice yoga poses. If you can literally feel your intention within the physicality of your practice, you are fully experiencing it. You could even say you are embodying it. It will create meaning in your practice and shifts in your life.

To set an intention that can be fully felt in your body, set it based on an action or actions that are physical within your yoga practice and also have meaning and application in your life. For example, many yoga poses require an action of anchoring. You might feel there's an area of your life where you need to be more anchored so your practice would be focused on this anchoring action. Another example is ease. Almost all yoga poses require an amount of ease, with some requiring more ease than others; you may feel you need more ease in your life. In this case, you would explore finding the right amount of ease in poses. A number of poses require strength, and you could use this as a metaphor to find inner strength, recruiting strength where necessary in your practice. There are an endless number of actions that can be felt within the body and can be used to set an intention relevant to your day-to-day life: finding balance, expansion, steadiness, compassion, a sense of being grounded or energized to name but a few.

Play with just one intention so you can consistently thread it through your practice to be fully in your body. Make the embodiment of your intention as simple as possible by just focusing on a couple of actions that support the intention. This chapter offers four different intentions for your practice and shows how to thread the actions through two poses. Of the two poses, in some of the examples, one pose is quite different to the other. This is to illustrate how specific actions supporting an intention can be threaded through your entire practice to change the way you look at things.

Embody your intention

Intention: finding openness

Set an intention to be open in an area of your life where you might be closed to something. Being open will bring new perspectives and create the shift.

To give an example, a yoga teacher I know likes to practice on his front porch. Opposite his porch are two trees that block the sunlight. He'd really like to have the trees removed so he can practice in a space filled with sunlight, but other family members love the trees and want to keep them. When he practices with the intention of being open to other perspectives, he becomes open to the majesty of the trees, the birdsong coming from within them and the beauty the trees bring with the change of seasons. The intention creates shifts in his life.

TRIKONASANA

Trikonasana, with its long lines, expansion of the limbs and revolving of the heart is, by its very essence, an open pose. When you practice the pose with the actions of creating long lines and revolving the heart, it's likely you will experience a sense of openness. If that's not your experience, then it soon will be, even if you need to modify the pose in a way that suits your body type. Use Trikonasana to support an intention of finding openness in an area of your life.

Practice with open poses, such as Trikonasana, to support your intention of openness but explore finding openness in less-open poses too. Additionally, infuse your practice of Trikonasana and your practice as a whole with a mindful sense of openness in your body. It will reinforce your intention and create meaning. Here are some things for you to try in Trikonasana:

1. Position your feet and legs for entry into the pose, reach your arms into a star shape above your head and inhale a sense of openness into the shape. As you exhale, absorb the sensation.

2. To cultivate a sense of openness:

   - reach from your hips down through the feet

   - extend from the pelvis up through the crown of the head

   - extend from the heart past your fingertips.

3. Allow the exhale to guide an opening of the arms as you partially hinge at the hip. Hold the arms wide for a breath or two. Explore what in your body can open more. Perhaps there's room for further expansion in your arms and stretch through your fingertips.

4. Now move into the full expression of the pose. Open your heart to the sky. Be open to new possibilities.

PARIVRTTA PARSVAKONASANA

Continue with an intention of finding openness in your life when you practice Parivrtta Parsvakonasana. Typically, it may be harder to find the feeling of openness in this pose, but you can still find the long lines and turning of the heart open to the sky that cultivate a feeling of openness. Notice these are the same as the actions used for Trikonasana.

In this twisting pose, something magical happens when the hands press together in Anjali mudra. It ignites the twisting action and creates an openness in the chest. Although this pose is a closed twist, the irony is the pose can become very open when you commit your intention to your practice and practice with openness in your body.

Try the following in your practice of Parivrtta Parsvakonasana.

1. Begin in a low lunge with your back knee on the mat and prepare to twist. As you do so, hook the opposite elbow over your knee. The twist will likely feel closed at this point.

2. Inhale and press between your palms. Sense the top of the chest lengthen and the heart space begin to twist open.

3. Exhale and begin to infuse the pose with a sense of openness.

4. Now lift your back knee. To cultivate a sense of openness:

   - reach from your hips down through your back leg

   - extend from the pelvis up through the crown of the head

   - press the palms together to lift and open your heart space.

5. With each breath, as you twist, focus on finding openness. Be curious. Explore subtle changes to infuse the pose with your intention. Perhaps the belly needs to draw in more or you need to find more length in the spine in order to twist the heart open to the sky.

6. Find a full sense of openness in your heart as you open to new possibilities.

Intention: feeling centered

Set an intention to bring a perspective of being centered in an area of your life that feels scattered or disjointed. Feeling centered is about finding the space in the middle between two or more things. It's a point of reference between opposites, a place of reassurance or comfort that you can return to time and time again.

To give an example, a friend has a senior role in a large company.

She is also raising a young family. The personal and professional demands placed upon her are great, with her company often wanting her to work long hours. She is a dedicated yogi with a regular home practice. When she practices with the intention of being centered in her life, she explores finding balance between her work and family lives. Through the aim to feel centered, she feels inspired to manage her working hours in a way that maximizes family time. She discovered that her work life is teaching her to embrace family life, and this has made her feel more centered. This changed perspective has been a powerful force in shaping her life. She's placed boundaries around her working hours, which her colleagues have come to respect.

CAT COW

With cow pose, there is an expansion and extension of the front body as the heart lifts. With cat pose, there's a contraction of the front body as the head and pelvis draw in. By their very nature, the final shapes of cat and cow are opposites. Being able to see clearly these two opposites is an opportunity to find the center place. The opposing physical actions in a good practice of moving between the two shapes are hugging in to the center and a rooting action to lift up. These actions move in different directions but center the pose.

Use the two shapes and the two actions in your practice of cat cow to inspire a feeling of centeredness in a situation where you feel pulled in two different directions. Try the following.

1. Deliberately place your hands underneath your shoulders. They are the anchors of your intention to be more centered in an area of your life.

2. Start by moving slowly and softly between cat and cow. Take your time. Welcome every sensation.

3. Now actively root your palms into the mat as you come into cat. Notice how the rooting action creates lift in the spine as it rounds, making the shape feel stable and centered.

4. Now move into cow, with a strong drawing in of your belly. Be aware of how this stabilizes the back in its extended shape, making it feel supported and centered.

5. Enjoy the familiar journey of moving between cat and cow; a place of centeredness, just as my friend gained a sense of centeredness between her work and family lives.

VRKSASANA

Vrksasana, when balance can be found, is a pose that inspires a feeling of centeredness. When you practice this pose, it's likely you'll wobble some or even fall out of it. Yet, in the moments when you find balance, you'll mostly likely achieve this when you anchor through your standing foot to rise up through the crown of your head. These are two opposing actions, which create centeredness in the pose. Another is to hug the foot into the standing leg and the standing leg into the foot in order to create an upward lift. The pose is also a metaphor for returning to your center during wobbly times.

Try the following with Vrksasana (with an option to place a hand on the wall for added support).

1. Feel the steady support of the earth underneath your foot as you come into Vrksasana.

2. Place one or both hands on your heart. Breathe into this space. It's the center of your being.

3. Now, as you inhale, strongly root through your standing foot to feeling a drawing up through to the crown of your head. As you exhale, allow the feeling of being centered to land in your body.

4. On your next inhalation, press the foot into the leg and the leg into the foot. Notice the effect this has in lengthening the pose upwards. As you exhale, find a feeling of centeredness.

5. As you root down and hug in, feel a lift of energy from the waist upwards through your heart. Find the space between the opposite actions to feel centered.

Intention: finding space

Set an intention to find space in an area of your life that feels restricted. Perhaps you feel you need to slow down, create more time to think or place boundaries around someone or something. Finding some space will bring new perspectives and create the shift.

To give an example, a client, by her own admission, is very anxious and easily stressed. She has a lot going on in her life, with a full-time job, a busy household with children, her mother and her husband. She also has some ongoing health issues. She would argue frequently with her husband over minor things, which added to her stress. She then took up yoga and created space for herself in a private practice once a week. She valued carving out space for the practice and felt better for it. After some months passed, she felt that the space she was creating in her body enabled her to find more space in her mind. At the end of one practice, during Savasana, she had a light-bulb moment, realizing she had to let go of the small things that she would argue over with her husband. Not only did she find space in her life to practice yoga, but the practice of yoga also gave her the space to create a shift in her marriage.

ADHO MUKHA SVANASANA

In Adho Mukha Svanasana, there is a lengthening of the spine. There is also the action of breathing to create space. Use the expansive, space-creating qualities of the in-breath to infuse your practice. Use these two actions within the pose to support an intention of finding space in your life.

Here are some things for you to try in your practice of Adho Mukha Svanasana.

1. Move into the pose and focus on your breath. Take a full breath in and feel an expansion in your body. Exhale completely to make space for your next in-breath.

2. As you press through your hands, draw your ribs in and your belly in. Notice how this creates more length in your spine.

3. Lengthen your hips away from your hands so you feel your spine lengthen.

4. Now focus on moving the tops of the thigh bones back. Broaden across the tops of your thighs.

5. Stretch your spine long to lift your hips. Reach your hips up, moving into the space.

ARDHA DHANURASANA

Continue the intention to find space in an area of your life with Ardha Dhanurasana. Although the spine is in extension, rather than in the flexion of Adho Mukha Svanasana, it is nonetheless a pose where the spine needs to lengthen so that the pose culminates in a lift of the heart, creating spaciousness at the top of the chest. It's also a pose where space is needed around the lower back.

Try this as you practice Ardha Dhanurasana to cultivate a sense of space in your body and in your life.

1. Reach for one of your ankles and, as you take a full inhale, lift into the pose.

2. Lengthen your spine by extending the knee away from your pelvis and by moving the shoulder forwards of your pelvis. It's these opposing actions that create length in your spine. Do this in a way that creates space in your lower back.

3. Lift your heart forwards and upwards. Observe the space this creates in the front of your body.

4. Using the expansive quality of the in-breath, reach your heart and your bound ankle away from one another to create space in your body.

Intention: being humble

Set an intention to be humble in an area of your life. Being humble is about self-reflection, modesty and even putting others first. It's about being in service to yourself in a nurturing way or to others. We tend to get very caught up in our own opinions, but when we take time to serve, it reciprocates by giving a broader perspective and pulls us out of our set ways and views. When we serve humbly, the tension can melt away. *The way you look at things is the most powerful force in shaping your life.*

If you find yourself becoming a little self-centered or you feel as if you lack something within, practice with an intention of being humble. It's likely you will be able to clear the negative feelings. A common tendency is to fill your life with doing things, seeking success, but often what is needed is to clear out the negative feelings in order to feel more fulfilled. Do this with a humbleness practice.

The action of bowing forward supports an intention to be humble. Bowing down is a symbol of deep respect.

Breathing into the back of the body is also a way to embody the intention. The back of the body is the unknown, yet-to-be discovered side of you. It's the side that is full of untapped potential or it represents holding on to something that needs to be unlocked before you can move on. Channel the in-breath to the back of your body to be in service to yourself, acting with humbleness as you self-reflect and find new pathways.

BALASANA

In Balasana, there is a humble bowing down. When you take this pose in your practice, you are in service to yourself, recognizing the need for a few quiet moments. In those moments, you let go of your outer ego and practice with an attitude of humbleness.

Try the following in your practice.

1. If you like, use props to make your practice of Balasana completely comfortable.

2. Place a blanket underneath your forehead so it's softly supported. This enables you to bow fully with unfettered humility.

3. Move into the pose with your favorite restorative placement of the arms. Take a breath in, expanding into your back. As you exhale, bow to gravity and the humble qualities within you.

4. As you continue to bow forward, find a sense of introspection. Soften your body and let go. Let go of your individuality. It's likely you'll experience a sense of relief.

5. The forehead-earth connection is the point of humility; infuse your entire being with humbleness.

6. Notice how this pose allows for a letting go of yourself. Paradoxically, you may feel you gain a deeper connection to yourself.

PASCHIMOTTANASANA

Yogis tend to have a wide range of experiences with Paschimottanasana, this being a pose about the west side of the body, meaning the back body in yoga. Some find forward folding uncomfortable in the lower back and/or hamstrings, others feel stuck in the pose and frustrated at their lack of progress to go deeper, whereas others find it easy to surrender into its shape. The way you look at things is the most powerful force in your life. Whatever your experience, accept where you are in your practice of the pose and let go of any striving or effort. Be humble and let Paschimottanasana open your back body.

Try practicing Paschimottanasana as follows.

1. As you sit in Dandasana and prepare to bow forward, spend a moment thinking about whether there's anything you can do to cultivate the feeling of humbleness. For example, if you need

to, modify the pose by sitting on some blocks and/or have your head resting on the tall end of a bolster. Being more comfortable will help cultivate a sense of humbleness. You are being humble towards yourself.

2. Now burrow your heels into the mat and notice if that creates length in your back.

3. As you exhale, bow forward and cloak the shape with humbleness.

4. Breathe into the back of your body and surrender to where you are right now.

5. Use these moments in the pose to draw inwards. Notice how you feel from an internal place, letting go of your outer ego in order to be humble.

New perspectives to inspire your clients

When you have an intention that a creates shifts in your life, you have a meaningful experience that you might want to share in the classes you teach. This can be a powerful force in the way you plan classes. Draw on elements of your intention setting. Use the actions that you have felt in your body to support your intention. Articulate poses in a way you have experienced them. Wrap what you draw from your personal practice into a theme. This is a great example of how having an established home practice can truly support you.

The chances are that personal content shared with your clients will resonate; they will be inspired. You'll be bringing a different perspective to the way they see things. They will recognize the authenticity in you, which will also be a powerful force in shaping your life.

Summary

- Set an intention for your home practice that you can feel in your body, which, in turn, can support you in your day-to-day life. You need to be able to fully embody your intention.

- Identify physical actions for your practice that support your intention. The actions need to have some universal application to your practice so that you can practice the actions in a range of poses.

- The actions should represent your intention, either literally or metaphorically.

- You may or may not normally practice in this way. However, fully feeling your intention in your practice will bring new perspectives, which can be a powerful force in shaping your life.

- As a teacher, you can draw from your own practice and intention setting and bring these into the classes you teach. You'll be bringing new perspectives to your clients, which will be a powerful force in shaping their lives too.

— *Chapter 7* —

SAME POSE, NEW SHAPE

Now for some fun. In this chapter, we take a pose and look at whether it can be practiced in other ways to give vitality and variation to your practice. By exploring variations, you are being creative in your practice, which is a bridge to being creative in your life. John O'Donohue said: "When we are creative, we help the unknown to be known, the invisible to be seen and the rich darkness within us to become illuminated."

Creativity brings the gift of seeing things from different perspectives; it brings an attitude of flexibility. It illuminates the known and unknown darkness within you. The known darkness is the one we experience during difficult times. The unknown darkness is the potential within us. *Creativity is a way to illuminate that darkness*, lighting it up so it becomes something magical and meaningful to you.

Your practice is a progression, and it's only by practicing that you can find the invisible shapes; the creativity is already within you. You'll find new shapes, new transitions, new patterns of breathing, thinking and feeling. You'll bring a new creative level to the way you experience yoga on your mat and in your life. It'll also bring more joy and variation to your teaching.

You may find it easy to be creative and see a pose in a different form. Or perhaps you are able to practice in an intuitive way to find new poses from the same shape. If that's not your experience, pause to think of the many possibilities of practicing a pose in a different way. For example, Utthita Hasta Padangustasana, when the raised leg is held out to the side, is, effectively, Trikonasana standing on one leg.

Sometimes a structured way of looking at things is the key to unlocking the door to creativity. It's likely you'll be able to practice a pose in at least two, if not more, of the following ways.

- Prone on the front of the body.

- Supine on the back body.

- On all fours.

- Seated.

- Kneeling.

- Inverted.

- Standing.

- If the pose has more than two points of contact with the mat, look at whether it can be practiced with fewer points of contact or with different parts of the body connecting to the mat.

- Explore if the pose can become a balance.

It's also useful to think about the direction of shapes and movement, as it might be possible to vary these with some shapes. For example, many poses can morph into a twist or a lateral shape. The amount of effort applied to a shape can, to a degree, also change its shape. It will certainly change your experience. You can experiment with taking a passive pose and making it active. Or you can move part or all of your body in the pose, perhaps swaying or circling, bending or straightening or moving forwards and backwards. Engaging with the breath, of course, can completely change your feeling in a pose.

Simply think about doing a pose in an opposite way. For example, if the pose is one that is bound, like Gomukasana arms, then don't bind. Do it differently, create the shape, keeping the arms very active but without the bind. This pose is usually held, so move in it, either bound or unbound. Sway sideways, forwards and backwards. Gomukasana is often practiced seated or standing, so you could do the opposite and practice it in Balasana.

Accessing your creativity doesn't just come from practicing a pose very differently. Small variations can feel profound. For example, in Virabhadrasana 2, you can vary the pose by turning your palms up or placing your hands on your heart. You'll likely find these types of small variations completely change how you feel in the pose and will inspire new movement into your next pose.

This chapter provides examples of how you can take a pose and recreate the shape in a different way. The variations are by no means limited to the ones offered here. There will be others that you already know and others you will discover in your own practice. The aim is to be playful, curious and safe, particularly if you are exploring stronger variations or are working with an injury. Take a shape, be innovative and weave it through your practice.

Cat cow

The rippling motion of cat and cow has so many possibilities. Often, it's just used at the beginning of a practice as a warm up, but you can easily base an entire practice around it. It's possible to practice cat cow at almost every level from supine to standing. You can also use it to inspire more dynamic movement. Here are a few ideas for you to try and, as you do so, extend from the core of your body with light shining out to *illuminate your practice.*

From an all-fours position

Cat cow is typically practiced from all fours. You could vary this by lifting your knees off the mat by a few inches. Notice how the movements of cat and cow become much smaller; it's as if you are engaging with the darkness within you.

You'll be familiar with a whole raft of variations in cat cow where a leg and/or an arm is extended. One variation to try is to extend a leg up and away from you, for cow pose, and then draw the knee to the outside of the shoulder for cat pose. You can even extend the leg out to the side.

Now as you move between cat and cow, begin to follow your intuition, be creative and move into less familiar places.

Seated or kneeling with varying degrees of effort

Have your arms in a cactus shape and move between extension and flexion. Start by moving slowly and softly and then increase the effort until you feel as if the movement is wading through a heavy liquid. You'll soon begin to feel some heat in your body. Incorporate a lion's breath when you move into cat, and release your creativity.

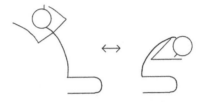

Prone on your belly in Salamba Bhujangasana

Set yourself up in Salamba Bhujangasana. Cow pose, in this variation, is Salamba Bhujangasana with the heart shining out. The cat shape comes from rounding through your upper back through to your shoulders, neck and head, moving in towards your darkness. If you'd like to make the cat aspect more dynamic, explore lifting the tops of your thighs off the mat with a strong engagement of your abdominals. This added effort will change your experience in the pose from semi-passive to strong and fiery. Ask yourself which of these variations illuminates the dark places of your body so they can shine out with creativity.

Standing

In your practice, explore standing posture variations of cat cow. One example is from Virabhadrasana 1 with the hands clasped behind your back. You can flow between cow, with a lift of the chest, into a humble warrior, this being a cat variation. Root strongly through your feet in order to explore the full range of motion between cat and cow in this variation. Allow the spine to ripple. In this standing version, notice how the range of motion is greater as you move from being extended with the heart lifted to fully bowing down. Notice whether this range of movement inspires a sense of creativity.

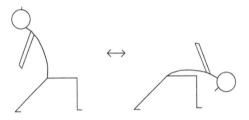

Flowing

You can move more dynamically with cat cow inspired shapes. This cat cow movement naturally occurs in sun salutations. It is the creative movement between extension and flexion, which is at the core of yoga itself.

From Balasana (cat inspired), staying low, you can snake forward into Bhujangasana (cow inspired) and back again into Balasana.

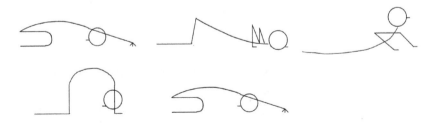

From Adho Mukha Svanasana (cow inspired), round the upper back and move forwards into a slightly curved high plank (cat inspired).

Bend your knees and push back into a hovering Balasana (cow inspired) and then, on your journey back to Adho Mukha Svanasana, find a small amount of flexion in your back as you would in cat pose before moving into the full expression of Adho Mukha Svanasana (cow inspired). You could also experiment with reversing this rippling flow.

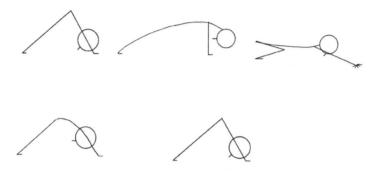

For a strong inspired version of cat cow, take Vashistasana. Create a cat-pose shape by bringing your top knee and elbow to meet in front of you. Create a cow shape by moving the foot and arm behind, reaching or tapping your fingers towards the sole of your foot. Here you are taking gentle shapes and are activating them with your creativity to create a completely different experience.

Vrksasana

Like cat cow, there are many tree-inspired shapes you can create in your practice. As you do so, explore how illuminated the shapes make you feel.

Supine variations

At the beginning of a practice, you could start by lying on your back and slide your foot along the inside of your leg into a supine Vrksasana. Take your arms overhead. Breathe and relax into the passive shape. This opens your practice with an acknowledgement of Vrksasana. Then change your experience by making the shape much more active: flex the foot of the "standing" leg and stretch your fingertips away. You are lengthening through your whole body.

Then bring the knee across the body with the opposite hand into a tree inspired twist.

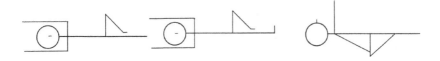

Tree can also be practiced prone on your belly, moving into Salamba Bhujangasana and illuminating your heart.

Standing variations

Once you are in Vrksasana, experiment with bending the knee of the standing leg and then straightening it as you come to rise onto the ball of your foot. This takes a balancing pose to another level of balance.

Twist in your traditional version of Vrksasana. Open the arms to shoulder height as you twist towards the bent knee. Then twist to the opposite side. Notice which side challenges your balance more.

Equally, try lateral stretches in Vrksasana, taking small stretches to both sides and noticing how this affects your balance. As you come back to center, notice how nicely familiar that place feels. The question you can ask yourself as you play with these forms is this: is your creativity starting to flow? Creativity flowing through you is more important than the shape.

Dynamic variations

Begin in Adho Mukha Svanasana and bring one leg into a tree shape. Stabilize in this shape, move forward into a "tree" plank and then back again into a "tree" Adho Mukha Svanasana. Notice how this horizontal version of Vrksasana is challenged by gravity. Notice which of the two poses feels more luminous: the "tree" plank or "tree" Adho Mukha Svanasana.

Inverted variations

Take some fun tree-leg variations to your inversion practice.

Trikonasana

Before looking at a number of variations, begin with the usual practice of Trikonasana and examine the placement of the lower hand. Whether you place that hand on your shin, on a prop or all the way to the floor, you can change the experience of the pose by placing less weight on that hand. Change the connection of the full hand to just one fingertip or fully float the hand. It's reaching to find the *invisible* within you.

In another variation, try placing the hand of the top arm behind your head and extend the elbow forwards (not upwards). Now press your head into your hand. This pressing action requires effort, but you'll connect more with the darkness of the back body as it lengthens into your hand.

Supine

Practice Trikonasana propped up on your side. This fun, simple variation can feel like a balance. If it doesn't, be playful and try lifting the leg resting on the mat by a few inches.

Supta Padangusthasana is a fully supine version of Trikonasana if you practice with the leg externally rotated as you take it out to the side. Tune in to the shape; it can feel very open and *luminous*.

Kneeling

Parighasana, you will know; it's a kneeling version of Trikonasana with the extended leg slightly internally rotated if you have the toes of that leg pointing forwards. Try the second kneeling version, where the straight leg in Parighasana is bent and externally rotated, and compare the luminosity in the two poses. You might find the ability to revolve the heart space is the same in both. With the second variation, you'll likely feel a greater sense of luminosity because the external rotation of the leg permits a wider range of lateral movement from the hip. Try both versions and tune in to your own experience.

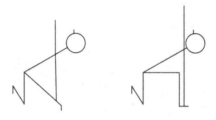

Lateral planks

Have fun with plank versions of Trikonasana and explore progressively stronger variations. Fallen triangle is a Trikonasana-inspired shape that can be practiced with the foot on the mat or hovering off the mat. Or be more aligned with the original pose and practice (or work towards) Vashistasana B. Engage with your creativity to practice these more challenging variations of the same pose to create a new shape.

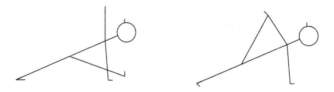

Adho Mukha Svanasana

Tap into your creativity to practice this quintessential yoga pose in some non-quintessential ways. Discover some unknown shapes and make them known within your practice.

Different mat contact points

You'll be familiar with changing your downward facing dog to a forearm dog, but you could try practicing the pose on your fingertips to strengthen the wrists. Or you could alter the placement of your hands, perhaps turning them out. You can move in the pose, altering the points of contact between the soles of your feet and the mat. You can come onto the balls of your feet or lift your toes. You can also move to the edges of your feet, with or without a slight bend of the knees. Be creative as you move to explore these variations and make new discoveries of your own.

Seated

If you reach your arms over your head in Navasana, this creates an inverted Adho Mukha Svanasana. You'll likely find this variation more challenging, as the lines of the shape move wide of your foundation and defy gravity. Notice whether the luminous appearance of the shape reflects your internal experience of this shape.

Standing

Take the standing pose of Parsvakonasana and fuse it with the flexion of Adho Mukha Svanasana to create a new shape.

Or take Prasarita Padottanasana but walk the hands as far in front of you as you can to create a wide-legged Adho Mukha Svanasana.

Inverted

You can replicate the "V" shape of Adho Mukha Svanasana with a pike press into Salamba Sirsasana. To some extent, you can also replicate the shape in Halasana, where the torso and legs are in the shape of a "V." *The way you look at things is a powerful force in shaping your life.*

Ardha Dhanurasana

The expansive quality of the in-breath assists with the lengthening of the spine in Ardha Dhanurasana but the paradox is that the breath can also become labored in this pose. It's a strong pose because of its asymmetrical shape, relying on the strength of the muscles of the back to defy gravity, lift and create space in the body. Try the following variations and compare the new shapes to the original pose. See where they take you. You might find, for example, that many of the variations can be practiced as a twist with the foot bound by the opposite hand.

Prone

Try practicing Ardha Dhanurasana by taking the advanced shape of the pose with the arm externally rotated above the head but without connecting the hand to the foot.

Try another prone variation, again without connecting the hand to the foot. In this variation reach the hand back as if you are going to hold your knee, moving laterally, and then lift as you would in the usual pose.

Or you can practice Ardha Dhanurasana as usual, but with both hands holding the lifted foot. As you lift and shine your heart forwards, feel your creativity glow.

Kneeling variations

It's likely you'll find the kneeling variations of Ardha Dhanurasana easier to practice than the traditional pose. There is a broader base of support.

Begin the following kneeling variation in a kneeling side plank. Bend the knee of the lifted leg, draw the foot behind using the strength of your back muscles and then reach for the foot with your hand.

Now try the Ardha Dhanurasana shape in Ardha Ustrasana. In this version, the back is moving towards the mat rather than away from it. You will notice more activation in the thighs. As you revolve your heart to the sky, ask the unknown within you to become known.

A progression from Ardha Ustrasana is a semi-kneeling version. It is less stable, but ask yourself whether the ability to balance with the heart shining upwards illuminates something within you, *making the invisible seen.*

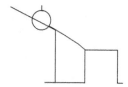

Lateral plank

Taking Ardha Dhanurasana in a plank position is challenging. As you focus on balancing in this strong shape, can the creativity within you continue to flow?

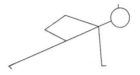

Balancing

Two notable balancing variations of Ardha Dhanurasana are Chapasana and Natarajasana. There are some further balancing variations that also happen to be kneeling variations. Try these.

The first variation is a simple same-side bind.

In the second variation, the right arm slides underneath you until the side of the head comes to the mat. Slowly extend the left leg with the toes on the mat and then lift the leg. If you feel steady enough, bend the knee and reach for the foot with your left hand. You might roll out, so ensure the area around you is clear. Have some fun in the same pose but with a new shape.

Paschimottanasana

Paschimottanasana is a pose that, perhaps, has the fewest direct variations. Use this as an opportunity to explore less obvious, more subtle variations. Engage with your creativity. Twist some. Experiment with the placement of your hands as you breathe into the back of your body and bow down with a quality of humbleness. You could even take a moving cat cow version. Ripple the spine from Dandasana in a cow shape with the heart shining forwards, into Paschimottanasana, and then back up into Dandasana through a cat-inspired movement.

Standing variations

Uttanasana, Ardha Uttanasana and Utthita Hasta Padangustasana (particularly the variation where the foot of the raised leg is held with both hands and the torso is folded forward towards the leg) are clear direct variations, but you can find others using movement to diversify your practice. Explore Uttanasana on your heels or the balls of your feet or with one knee slightly bent. Twist or move your hips to the side. Experiment with the placement of your hands and/or move your arms into different positions. Gomukasana arms or placing your hands in reverse Anjali mudra might be possibilities for you in your practice. If that's not the case, place your hands on the wall for Ardha Uttanasana and explore your variations from there. Start moving, even if in small ways, to get your creativity flowing.

Inverted and seated

Halasana is an inverted variation of the pose. A simpler variation is to have your legs stretched over your head (possibly with a bend in your knees) with the lower back and hips remaining on the mat.

Navasana is a balancing variation that you can practice by holding your feet or legs to create the Paschimottanasana shape. Or you could try rolling between the two poses, just for fun.

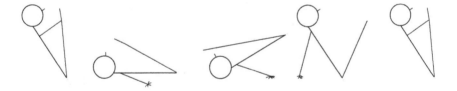

Creativity is within you even if it may not feel that way. Sometimes it can be clouded by life in general. If you begin to move in your body, breathing life into the smallest of movements, you will gain access to your creativity. Let go of the form in your practice to find it. Begin with simple, familiar movements and then follow your intuition. Use your creative self to bring new awareness into the rich darkness that is within you, just as the darkness of winter and all that is dormant underground become the beauty of spring. Access your creativity to illuminate your practice and your life.

Summary

- Yoga poses are about creating shapes that symbolize something and have meaning. Take a shape and thread it through your practice just as you thread the breath throughout your practice.

- Creativity resides within you and you can access it by moving. You will likely find a yoga pose can be recreated in many different ways, from supine to standing to upside down. Just get on your mat and move to explore a pose in its many different shapes.

- As you move, be attuned to where and how your body wants to move. Be less concerned with good form and more concerned with accessing your creativity. Just let your practice be free.

- Practicing with creativity is a way to grow your practice. You'll make new discoveries about yourself and it will illuminate your practice and your teaching.

Chapter 8

MOVEMENT IS YOUR PATH

Your practice, your work

In the words of Ram Dass (in *Be Here Now*), "Start from where you are—not where you wish you were. The work you are doing becomes your path," so start from where you are right now and move. The body loves to move and there are many amazing ways it can do so. The more you move, and the more you move differently, the more adaptable and resilient your body can become. In yoga, creating shapes and moving is a gateway to a deeper connection between your breath, mind and body. As the body ages, movement becomes particularly important. There are so many good reasons to move, so start with where you are in your practice. Your practice is your work but *allow movement to become your path*. This chapter offers ways to vary how you move from one shape to another to *create new paths in your life*.

A new path brings new opportunities. To change your path, you need to do something different, perhaps take something away to add something new. Or take a completely different perspective. To give an example, when I was a child, I trained as a competitive gymnast. Training was most evenings from 6pm to 9pm and seven hours each day at the weekend. For a nine- to ten-year-old, that was a tough path to be on. During the day, I had no interest in school. I was fatigued. In fact, I resisted going to school. My parents despaired of me. It was a grim situation. In my mind, gymnastics was all that I identified with; it was my life. Going to school was not a path I wanted to take. At the age of 11, I was due to move from junior school to secondary school. During the summer vacation, when schools were closed, I had a complete change of perspective. I realized I needed to drop my ambition of being an international competitive gymnast; I had to focus on my education. When the school path temporarily closed, I realized that was the path to be on. The changed perspective opened up a world of education, better friendships and time to devote to new hobbies. One path closed, but others opened up.

My intention in sharing this story is to show how significant shifts can occur when you make changes to the path you are on. Special, meaningful and transformative things can occur. You don't have to leave your previous path permanently, just explore new ones and see where they take you. Do this through the movement in your yoga practice—it is your work—and allow it to be a metaphor for the paths that life takes you down.

Sun salutations

In most dynamic yoga practices, sun salutations are used to transition through a series of sequences, with Adho Mukha Svanasana being the key pose through which sequences often begin. The symbolism of a sun salutation is important in yoga because of the reminder to practice towards the rising sun in the east, this being a metaphor for honoring the light that is within you. Also, the physical movements of a sun salutation, moving between shapes of extension and flexion, are a metaphor for the interplay of the light and the darkness within you. Sun salutations are heating and healthy for most body types, creating strength and flexibility. The comforting familiarity of a sun salutation, which is akin to a trusted, well-walked path, enables a practice to become more of moving meditation. You can go deeper in your work knowing the path you are on.

However, imagine a world of yoga without sun salutations or even without Adho Mukha Svanasana. We'll look at these ideas later in the chapter. Or imagine a different type of sun salutation. One that is less familiar to you or one that you have created or varied from your usual practice. This chapter is not suggesting you drop the sun salutations that feature regularly in your practice. Instead, it offers a different way to practice on occasions, because sometimes we need to take a different path.

Vary your sun salutation

Get on your mat and experiment with varying your sun salutation. Start from where you usually are, in Tadasana, and explore how you might vary the familiar path. You could stay with the same shapes but make some small changes. Small changes can make a big difference. Or you could swap out usual poses in your salutation for other yoga poses.

Here are a few ideas to try for varying sun salutation A.

- Vary Urdhva Hastasana by rising up onto the balls of your feet with your hands interlaced above your head. Do this to challenge your balance.

- Vary Uttanasana by interlacing your hands behind your back to stretch your shoulders. You could also try remaining on the balls of your feet as you do this.

- For Ardha Uttanasana, take a small bend in your knees and bring your arms up behind your back, adopting a ski jump shape. Squeeze the muscles around your shoulder blades.

- Hold Chaturanga Dandasana (or plank) for a couple of breaths. As you do so, move your body a little to the left and then to the right to strengthen your arms, shoulders and abdominals.

- Instead of Urdhva Mukha Svanasana, take a different backbend. You could take a Salabhasana variation. For example, you can interlace your hands behind your back and aim to tap one foot, and then the other, on your interlaced fingers.

- Take one of the Adho Mukha Svanasana variations offered in the previous chapter, or you could twist by placing one hand on the opposite shin and then switch sides.

- When you jump to the front of your mat, jump forwards into a standing split. Or walk your hands to the back of your mat for a change.

- Vary the placement of your hands or arms in Uttanasana. For example, you could hug your arms around the backs of your knees or walk your hands from one side and then to the other side to take a small twist.

- Rise up into Urdhva Hastasana on the balls of your feet and then settle into the familiarity of Tadasana.

Now vary the sun salutations in your practice. Tap into your creativity. That's the work that becomes your path.

Create a new sun salutation

As part of your work, invent a new sun salutation for your practice. It'll open doors of creativity as well as helping you to find new paths. Start with the framework of moving between extension on an inhalation and flexion on an exhalation and see where your body takes you. Begin in a neutral pose, such as Tadasana, kneeling or Svanasana, and build your sequence from there. You could give your sun salutation a particular focus: supine, lateral, balancing or symmetrical, for example. Or you could aim to make your sun salutation quite gentle, such that it's practiced with much support from the ground, or you could make it strong and challenging, incorporating inversions and heating poses.

The simplicity of building a short sequence based on extension and flexion gives a real opportunity to be inventive. Here are a couple of sequences for you to try. The first is a kneeling sun salutation. Here, the movement is literally shortened, with the lower part of the legs remaining mostly connected to the mat. See if there's something to be gained in your practice by taking away the lower legs in the salutation. In the second, a different perspective, that being a lateral perspective, is brought to the sun salutation. Experiment to see whether a different perspective takes you on another path.

KNEELING SUN SALUTATION

1. Begin in a high kneeling shape with legs hip distance apart.

2. **Extension (inhale):** Raise your arms above your head.

3. **Flexion (exhale):** Cat pose.

4. **Extension (inhale):** Step into Anjaneyasana.

5. **Flexion (exhale):** Fold over your front leg.

6. **Extension (inhale):** Straighten your front leg, place your hands on the mat or on props and lengthen your torso forwards with your heart lifted.

7. **Flexion (exhale):** Fold over your front leg.

8. **Extension (inhale):** Step back into a high kneeling position and place the hands on the lower back for a supported Ustrasana.

9. **Flexion (exhale):** Low kneel.

10. **Extension (inhale):** Walk the hands back and lift the heart.

11. Return to high kneeling.

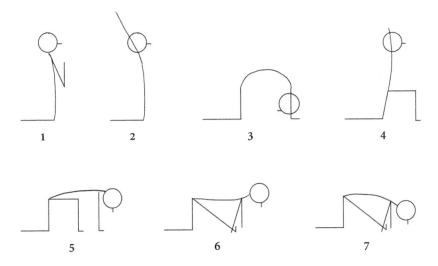

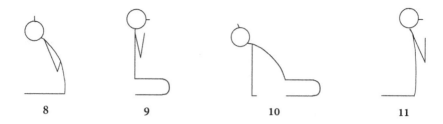

8   9   10   11

LATERAL SUN SALUTATION

1. Begin in Tadasana.

2. **Extension (inhale):** Step your right foot behind and to the left and stretch to your left, holding your right wrist with your left hand.

3. **Flexion (exhale):** Step your right foot wide out to the right, bend into the right knee and take your hands to the floor in a low side lunge with a soft bow forwards.

4. **Extension (inhale):** Lengthen your spine and extend your arms behind and above your back.

5. **Flexion (exhale):** Prasarita Padottanasana.

6. **Extension (inhale):** Utkata Konasana with your hands interlaced behind your back and heart lifted.

7. **Flexion (exhale):** Side stretch to the right in goddess pose with a small amount of flexion as if in cat pose.

8. **Extension (inhale):** Parsvakonasana, heart shines upwards.

9. Return to Tadasana.

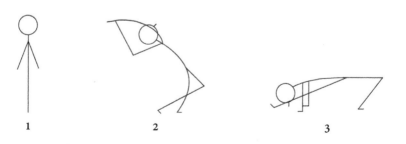

1   2   3

When you create your own sun salutations, you might find your sequences take you off the mat or away from the top of your mat. Give yourself the freedom to practice outside the four edges of your mat. *Move from where you are, not from where you wish you were.*

Be free to set your own parameters

When you come to your mat, set yourself some parameters within which to practice. Set the parameters in a way that will motivate you to move differently so that you create a new path. For example, you could set the parameter of not including a single Adho Mukha Svanasana in your practice. If you usually transition through Adho Mukha Svanasana, this parameter will force you to practice other transitions and discover some new ones.

Make setting your parameter a fun challenge for yourself. Take things that feature regularly in your practice and set the parameter of not including them. Or set your parameter to be the opposite of what commonly features in your practice—things you don't practice so much. Aim to discover new poses, practice less favored ones and find new ways to move.

Here are a few parameters you can try in your practice.

- Try a "no hands on the mat" practice. You'll need to explore different transitions, as it won't be possible to incorporate a typical sun salutation in your practice. Perhaps you will begin a sequence of standing postures by taking Virabhadrasana 3 from Tadasana and stepping back into a lunge. You could transition to the floor from Urdhva Hastasana on the balls of your feet, to a squat and then into Navasana. If your practice takes you back into a standing practice, stand up directly from Sukhasana or Ardha Matseyandrasana without the use of your hands.

- Try a supine practice. You could set an additional parameter of making it a strong practice, because being supine is often associated with resting or a softer practice. The practice could be strong in terms of incorporating differing poses that work the abdominals, work the glutes and hamstrings in bridge variations and heat the body in Urdhva Dhanurasana.

- Try a seated practice that permits small lifts from the floor. You can begin in Dandasana and explore some of your own variations in this pose. You can move through Purvottanasana and Navasana and lift your legs off the mat in an arm balance from Sukhasana. You can twist in Marichyasana 1 and lift into Camatkarasana and then forward fold in Janu Sirsasana.

- Try a standing practice where your feet are hip distance apart. You can take one foot off the mat to balance, but when you place your foot on the mat it has to be replaced back in its original position. Aside from exploring a range of standing balances, explore twisting, extending, moving laterally, circling your upper body and folding forward with your two feet firmly rooted to the ground. See how many new paths of movement you can find by standing still.

- Try a practice where you regularly move between standing postures and those that are supine or seated within each sequence so that you'll be moving in upward and downward directions. It's unlikely you would sequence a class in this way, but be experimental in your home practice to find a new path.

Your very own path

Previous chapters in this book have explored the power of intention, such that your practice and movement occur within the framework of your intention. Indeed, this is the work you are doing, and the mere fact of having an intention for your practice can make for deep work. If you regularly use intention in your practice then, paradoxically, you should practice without any intention and without any structure around some of your yoga practices. Come to your mat without any particular aim. Do not have a climax pose in mind. Don't aim to practice any particular groups of postures. Don't set an intention. Just begin from where you are and move freely. See how that feels. Practicing with unfettered freedom on some occasions can be a joy. *That might create a new path for you.*

Summary

- The greatest gift you can give yourself is presence, but moving your body is another great gift to yourself.

- Movement is not work, movement is your work.

- Experiment with moving in different ways. Seek less familiar movement in your practice; challenge yourself to make new discoveries.

- Find new movement by consciously practicing in a different way. Practice less favored poses; try different sun salutations or create your own.

- Finding new paths in your practice by moving in new ways is a metaphor for finding new paths in your life. You may need to do things differently in order to move from where you are.

Chapter 9

GETTING THE MOST FROM YOUR PRACTICE

Let yoga awaken your life

John O'Donohue describes a friend as, "a loved one who awakens your life in order to free the wild possibilities within you" in his book *Anam Cara*. I regard my yoga practice as my friend. It is something I am loyal towards, but my practice is also forgiving and understanding. You don't always have to be good in your practice, seek perfection in your alignment or come to your mat every day. Don't tire of something you love and don't feel guilty if you miss a practice you had planned for. My practice is supportive, like a friend, but it also awakens my life and helps to free the possibilities within me, just as a close friend does.

Some days, favor creativity in your practice over good form, just as we explored in the previous two chapters. Enjoy freedom of movement. Be spontaneous and favor this over good alignment if it helps to get you on your mat for a home practice.

On other days, find good form in the shapes you create and then let go of it. Soften and relax. Find a feeling of formlessness. Allow the pose to become something other than a physical shape. That might be an experience, something spiritual, a moment when something falls into place or simply a feeling of pure presence. Yoga is not about perfecting the pose. Above all, remember the spark within you and your reasons for practicing yoga; it's unlikely your reasons were about finding perfection in poses. Be curious and playful so that you can love your practice and *let your body move in a way that it loves.*

Yoga as a means of self-care

The mere practice of yoga is a means of self-care, a way to improve your well-being. You are breathing well and looking after your body and mind. You are feeling your practice with your whole being. You are more present. Within the practice itself, you know your body well, you are intention setting and using your practice as a means to support your life off the mat.

Within your practice, challenge yourself to slow down completely with the use of props to support you in a quiet, restorative yoga practice. Create the right conditions to be able to rest in this way. Let your body be soft and allow it to feel loved. Slowing down isn't a luxury. It is a necessity, especially if you feel as if you've been in overdrive. Or perhaps your emotional responses are overly strong, your immune system is at a low ebb or your breathing is shallow. Being in a state of deep relaxation releases muscle tension, produces feelings of tranquility and is rebalancing. It also gives a chance to focus and move inwards, something that may not be possible in a strong dynamic yoga practice.

Incorporate self-massage into your practice in poses where it is comfortable and accessible to do so. It can be soothing to massage your feet in Baddha Konasana, the tops of your legs in Dandasana or the back of your head in Uttanasana, for example. You might like to sit in a Dandasana shape, place a bolster across the tops of your thighs and fold forward so you are supported across your belly as you massage your toes and tops of your feet. You can also use massage balls to release tension in your back or where other muscles feel tight. Use these therapeutically. Releasing tension in muscles and fascia is relaxing and can provide relief if you experience pain. You'll become more familiar with the tighter areas of your body and can devote more attention to these in your home yoga practice.

Although there may be occasions when you need to slow down, it's likely there will be occasions when you need the opposite from your practice. Practicing strongly and intensively for short periods of time can improve cardiovascular fitness, which is also a form of self-care. If you are short on time, moving in a way that is strong and heating might be exactly what your body needs as part of a varied home practice.

Yoga is often viewed as a way to gain flexibility, which is true, but maintaining strength within your body is necessary on so many levels, not least for injury prevention. Strengthening muscles in a load-bearing way also helps to increase bone density. For example, take hops in Adho Mukha Svanasana to strengthen the bones of the arms and shoulders:

Devote some of your home practice to focusing on strengthening areas of your body that would benefit from this. That might include your glutes, abdominals or arms, for example. Strength is important in yoga because it supports you as you move. It can also support you as you stretch. If you are very flexible, maintaining strength is of particular importance to you. Whatever your flexibility, aim to build strength in your practice, whilst maintaining some softness, so you can *free the wild possibilities within you.*

When you practice yoga poses, it is likely that some part of your body will be stretched. Stretching is associated with flexibility. Having some flexibility is useful because it can increase the range of movement of your joints. This can be helpful in your day-to-day life as well as on your mat. It'll become important as your body ages. If you do not have a flexible body, but want a flexible body, have a good reason for seeking increased flexibility. Or change your view on being flexible. *Sometimes you need to know your limits in order to move beyond them.* It is possible to increase your flexibility over time but the extent to which you can do so depends on your genetic make-up, bone structure and commitment to increasing your flexibility on a regular basis.

If part of your self-care practice is to maintain or increase your flexibility, vary the ways in which you stretch. Many yoga poses involve stretching in a static way where the muscles are relaxed. Uttanasana, for example, is a static stretch of the backs of the legs, most notably the hamstrings. Static stretches are beneficial but you should also incorporate active stretches into your practice. Active stretches involve the engagement of muscles. An example is Eka Pada Rajakapotasana when practiced with the pelvic floor actively lifted a few inches away from the floor. Another example is in Anjaneyasana when practiced with the front foot and back knee actively hugging in to create a lift of the pelvis. Actively stretching not only builds strength, supporting your mobility as your flexibility increases, but also means you are less likely to overstretch.

Breathing is an integral part of a yoga practice on the mat but take those practices off the mat and into your daily life when you need them. The breath is truly one of the greatest resources we have. Take long inhales when you need to ground in a stressful situation. Focus on the releasing quality of the exhale to reduce anxiety. Take slow, deliberate breaths of even length to help find sleep. Take sharp inhales and exhales to energize. Explore what works for you. Make these breath interventions part of your daily self-care practice, and smile, they bring you into the present moment.

Injuries are opportunities

No one likes to be injured, but if you accept an injury when you have one, you can use it to deepen your knowledge of your body and of yoga. There is actually much to be gained from being injured. It can be human nature to ignore or work through injuries, often making them worse and prolonging recovery time. Injuries are inevitable, especially as the body ages, so use being injured as an opportunity to *know your limits so you can move beyond them. The way you look at things is a powerful force in shaping your life.*

The severity of an injury can range from tight and painful muscles to something more serious requiring a period of rehabilitation or even surgery. Whatever your injury, spend time researching and understanding what is happening in your body. Be familiar with what is injured. It might be a muscle, tendon or ligament, for example. If appropriate, seek advice on how best to treat the injury. Injuries often require a period of rest and/or heat or ice and many require rehabilitation exercises. If you need the intervention of a specialist, such as a physiotherapist, gain as much information as you can from that person to deepen your knowledge of the mechanics and anatomy of the injured area. Be familiar with the right course of action and also know what is not good for your injury. As you progress through your life as a yoga teacher, it's likely you'll come to know of specialists for particular types of injuries. Retain this knowledge and share it with your clients as and when it's appropriate.

Once you are armed with sufficient knowledge, learn how to adapt your practice to take account of your injury. You might need to change the focus of your practice, so use this as an opportunity to explore other avenues of your practice. For example, if you have a serious foot injury, change the focus of your practice to more breath-work and inverted, seated and supine poses. Not only that, listen to your body. *If you are quiet enough, you will hear* what it needs.

To give an example, a yoga teacher I know, after consulting with an orthopedic specialist, discovered she had a tear of the labrum in her hip joint. She used this as an opportunity to review the anatomy of the hip joint, including associated muscles, tendons and ligaments, some of which had become inflamed as a result of the tear. In doing so, and in consultation with her physiotherapist, she gained a more detailed understanding of how the hip joint aligns and what helps it to align appropriately. She was given a number of differing bridge exercises to practice, the aim of which was to strengthen her glutes to improve alignment of the joint. Taking this a step further, in her home practice, she explored other ways to strengthen her glutes by moving intuitively and listening to her body. In doing so, she discovered that movements that also strengthened the hamstrings helped significantly with reducing the pain of the injury and aligning the hip joint. These were small movements that she was able to incorporate into her teaching. In her own practice and through advice, she learned which poses aggravated the hip joint. There were some poses that felt good but would damage the joint in the long run. As a result, she avoided some poses altogether, practiced others with the support of props or didn't move into them as deeply. She took what, at the time, appeared to be a major injury and turned it into an opportunity to learn and support herself.

When you are able to make the most out of having an injury, you are able to use that awareness to support your clients. It would be wrong, of course, to assume that your experience of having a frozen shoulder, for example, is the exact same experience a client might be having. Yet, the knowledge you acquire enables you to be able to listen to your client, better understand their situation and suggest alternative shapes when appropriate. You might be able to introduce some movements into a general-level class that help with the rehabilitation of an injury which benefit all class participants. Your cuing will be more mindful, and you'll be building trust between you and your clients.

Fear of being injured can hinder movement and motivation to try new things. For example, fear might be around moving into inversions and/or arm balances to the point that certain poses are not practiced at all. Or there could be fear that certain movements might inflame an old injury. There may be good reason for the fear, yet, at the same time, place trust in your body because the body knows. Fear of things is often a learned behavior, so fear can be unlearned. Generally, the body has an innate way of protecting itself from injury. For example, if you fear falling out of a handstand but attempt one, you'll probably find your body will automatically twist into a half-cartwheel so that you come out of the pose with reasonable safety. If there's something you fear in your practice, take appropriate advice and/or build up to the pose safely with the support of props, regular practice and the appropriate amount of strength and flexibility the pose requires.

Draw from other disciplines

Make it part of your yoga practice to do non-yoga related activities or sports. Do other forms of exercise that your body loves: Pilates, barre, dance, parkour, running, climbing, team sports, etc. Draw on other disciplines to support your body and balance out your yoga practice, but also explore whether there are elements from other activities to incorporate into your home practice. Have the freedom to bring non-traditional yoga shapes and movements into your practice to enhance your practice. You might also find that as you engage in non-yoga forms of exercise, you value your home yoga practice even more.

Also, if you've lost your motivation to practice yoga, take a break from it. Yoga teacher training can be intense, and you might find you tire of yoga for a while. Or perhaps you are a busy teacher and feel a little burned out. Take a break from yoga and you'll find the motivation to practice will return very soon.

Your home practice is a ritual

Now that your home practice is fully established, it should feel like a cherished ritual in your life. A ritual is not just something you do; it is an embodiment of you. Be devoted to your practice such that you are practicing with the engagement of your whole heart. Your home practice is for you, so keep it separate from class planning and your teaching.

Perhaps place some ceremony around the way you come to your mat; do something that resonates strongly with you. For example, you might begin with a heart full of gratitude for your body and your practice, say a prayer, sing a mantra or make an offering. You might also close your practice in a similar way. Practice in a way that is special for you *in a way that will free the possibilities within you.*

Summary

- Seek creative and varied movement in your practice over perfection.

- Know what you need from your practice for it to be a self-care tool. That might be restorative yoga, self-massage or specific ways to build strength and maintain flexibility. Take your breathing practices off the mat to support you in your daily life.

- Avoid getting injured, but don't fear it. If you are working with an injury, use it as a learning experience to support yourself and your clients.

- Use non-yoga disciplines and sports to inspire different movement within your yoga practice. Moving in different ways is a form of self-care for your body.

- Allow your home practice to become a ritual. Be devoted to your home practice. Embody it and it will become part of who you are rather than something you just do.

—*Chapter 10*—

BRINGING IT ALL TOGETHER

Weaving tools into your practice

This final chapter is, in some ways, a little contradictory because it provides a sequence for you to practice when, in fact, a home practice is something for you to create and explore yourself. However, the aim here is to provide an illustration of how you can blend a range of topics covered in this book to enhance your practice.

Setting an intention is at the heart of this sequence. It's not only a way to create presence in your practice, but also a way to inspire and support yourself in life as a whole. Yoga is not just on the mat. It's a self-care tool and, if you choose, a way of life.

The intention is finding expansion in a contracted situation. It is inspired by an extract from Rumi's poem "The Guest House":

Be grateful for whoever comes,
because each has been sent
As a guide from beyond.

A friend shared this with me at a low point in my life. It's inspired me ever since, and I refer to it often. You can have the poem by your mat when you practice. It's a reminder to welcome the contracted times, which come as a guide. They may well lead to expanded times.

I use this intention when I can't see the positivity or possibility for growth in a situation that has affected me negatively. In life, we all constantly meet contracted situations, whether it's not getting along with a co-worker, struggling to be a good parent or a significant relationship break-up. It can be difficult to see the good in (what feels like) a bad situation; sometimes you have to look for it or be quiet in order to hear. To give an example, I experienced much grief when my mother endured a grueling illness and then died. However, over time, my relationship with my father deepened to a level I never thought possible. He and I have become extremely close, so much closer than when my mother was alive. It took me some time to see how this precious relationship grew from the contraction of illness, death and grief.

The sequence illustrates ways to maintain the intention. The first is to incorporate two actions, which can be felt in the body. One is to follow the breath, because it is a pulse between expansion and contraction, with a focus on the inhalation because of its expansive, awakening qualities. The second is the action of finding expansiveness in poses: stretching, lengthening and making a pose feel illuminated.

To support the intention and the action of finding expansiveness, I use a shape (or you could call it a mudra) that represents expansion to me. It's simply a shape of raising my arms above my head, a little wider than my shoulders, with my palms facing forwards and my fingertips extended. This mudra feels like expansion; I can experience that feeling in my body. It represents my intention and using it periodically throughout the practice helps maintain the intention.

The sequence itself includes moving between some contracted shapes and expansive shapes in the form of cat and cow variations. Cow pose involves the expansion of the front body and is a good preparatory pose for Ardha Dhanurasana, which requires a burst of expansion. The sequence also takes this pose and creates the shape in a few different ways, including a kneeling variation, Natarajasana and Ardha Bhekasana.

The practice also incorporates breath-work, meditation and energetics so you can sense with your whole body. Use all of these tools, and others, to hear messages sent by guides from beyond to enrich your life.

Before you begin the practice, identify the contracted situation you would like to expand from. Also allow yourself the freedom to vary elements of the practice to make it your own.

Sequence

Being present through breath-work

1. Lay on your back, soles of the feet on the mat underneath your knees, hip distance apart. Relax. Take a few deep breaths to drop into the physicality of your body.

2. Place one hand on your belly and the other on your upper chest and breathe. Notice where in your body you feel the expansion of the in-breath. After a couple of minutes, begin to make your in-breath a little longer than your out-breath. Remain here for a few more moments and imagine your breath is illuminating your entire body.

Warming up

1. Now stretch your arms over your head, turn your palms to face the ceiling and reach your fingertips away in the mudra symbolizing expansion. Lengthen your arms as you breathe in and then relax your arms as you breathe out. Focus on the sensation of expanding your upper body. Do this a few more times.

2. As you inhale, lift the hips into Setu Bandha Sarvangasana and lengthen your thighs. Lower down as you exhale. Do this a few more times and then hold the pose. Energetically, move your knees away from you and your heels towards your buttocks. Focus on the expansion of the tops of your thighs. Lower down

onto your back, roll to your side and come into Sukhasana resting your hands on your knees.

3. Expand into a seated cow pose and then contract into a seated cat pose. Using the breath to guide you, move between these two shapes of expansion and contraction.

4. Change the cross of your legs and take a yoga strap. Hold the strap in each hand wider than shoulder distance. Move the strap in front of you and then behind you, pausing at the point where you feel a stretch across the front of the chest. Do this a few more times until you feel an opening across the chest.

5. Come to a table-top position and then walk the hands forwards into Anahastasana. Explore this pose by taking some mini variations. Perhaps you come onto your fingertips or you take one arm back and then switch sides.

6. Take some Salabhasana variations, including a variation where your arms are extended in the mudra, and then rest. As you rest, take a moment to consider what expansion might feel like in the contracted situation you are faced with.

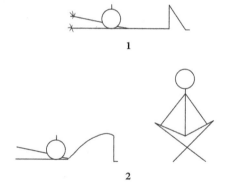

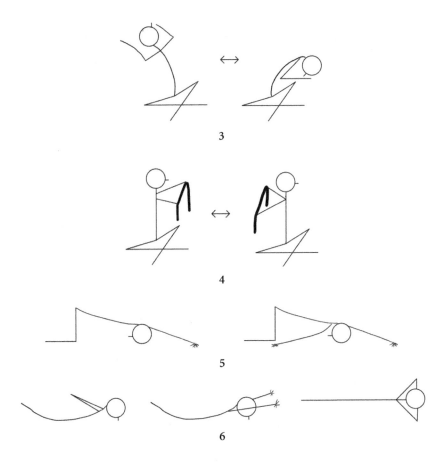

3

4

5

6

Sequence 1: practice on right and left sides

1. From a table-top position, move your lower left leg a little out to the left side and come into a kneeling side plank. From here, as you exhale, bring your right knee to meet your right elbow in front of you. As you inhale, aim to tap your right toes with your right fingers behind you. Move through these contracting and expanding movements a few more times.

2. Step your right foot between your hands and rise into Anjaneyasana. Now move between some cat and cow movements, and then return to Anjaneyasana. Lift through your heart, extend through

your arms and layer the pose with the mudra symbolizing expansion. Then move into Adho Mukha Svanasana.

1

2

Sequence 2: practice on right and left sides

1. Begin the sequence as you did in the first part of sequence 1. This time, when you tap your toes to your hand, take a bind and hold for a few breaths.

2. Step your right foot between your hands and rise into a high lunge. Lengthen from your waist up through your fingertips with the palms facing forward in the mudra. Take an in-breath and expand throughout your entire being.

3. Step into your front foot and come into Virabhadrasana 3 with your arms by your side. Lengthen. Now move into the contracted shape of standing on your right foot, drawing your left knee forwards and hugging it. Remember, the contracted situation is the springboard for expansion. Move between these two shapes a couple more times and then step back into a high lunge.

4. Take your left hand to the floor and elongate through your arms for an easy twist.

5. Step your front foot to meet your back foot in Vashistasana. From here, explore movements of expansion and contraction with your top arm moving upwards as you inhale and then under your lower waist as you exhale.

6. Now move into Adho Mukha Svanasana and then plank, and make your way onto the front of your body for Ardha Bhekasana with your right leg. Energetically move your bent knee away from you. Focus on the expansive qualities of your in-breath as you lengthen and expand your thigh. Then return to Adho Mukha Svanasana.

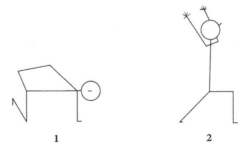

1   2

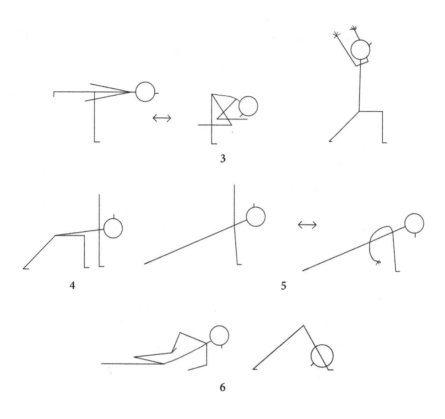

Sequence 3: practice on right and left sides

1. Find your way to Tadasana. Energetically, expand downwards through your legs and upwards through your torso. Breathe into your whole being, fill your body with your in-breath and raise your arms into the mudra.

2. Retain the expansive, energetic qualities you found in Tadasana as you stand on your right foot and catch the left foot with your left hand behind you. Lengthen the left knee towards the mat. After a few moments, lift the back foot and hinge forwards a little into Natarajasana.

3. Step the left foot back and come into a high lunge. Reach through the fingertips and expand beyond your being. Pause here and

tune in to what you are feeling. Then take Gomukasana arms. Lengthen the elbows away from one another.

4. Release into an easy twist, then into Adho Mukha Svanasana and then lower the knees to table top.

5. Take another Ardha Dhanurasana variation by lifting the right leg and right hand to bind. Expand slowly into the pose. Then rest in Balasana, welcoming these moments in the contracted shape.

6. Come onto the front of your body, take a deep breath in and move into Ardha Dhanurasana on the right side. Expand beyond your being as you lift into the pose. Use the breath to support you in the pose. Then rest. Ask yourself this: how can you expand from the contracted situation?

1 2 3

4

5 6

Sequence 4

1. Roll onto the back of your body. Hug a knee into your chest. Then press the knee into the hand and the hand into the knee to release the back. Switch sides.

2. Twist. Relax in the twist for a minute on each side. Use these moments to rest your awareness on your breath, being fully present in your practice.

3. From here, spend a few minutes in a seated meditation focusing on the expansive qualities of your breath. Place both hands on your heart. What can you find in your heart to grow or expand from the contracted situation in your life?

4. Savasana.

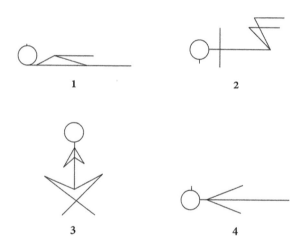

Your home practice is a guide from beyond

Yoga has a special way of touching your spirit, so always practice in a way that is magical for you. By exploring all or some of what is offered in this book, the intention is that your home practice will evolve into something that is very precious, supporting you both on and off the mat. Not only that, having an established home practice will also inform your teaching and make you stand out as a teacher. Your teaching will be original and authentic and come directly from your heart. Practice with a full heart, be grateful and it will be your guide.

GLOSSARY OF TERMS

Adho Mukha Svanasana: Downward facing dog

Anahastasana: Melting heart pose

Anjali mudra: Hands in prayer

Anjaneyasana: Kneeling lunge

Ardha Ananda Balasana: Half happy baby pose

Ardha Bhekasana: Half frog pose

Ardha Dhanurasana: Half bow pose

Ardha Matseyandrasana: Half Lord of the Fishes pose

Ardha Ustrasana: Half camel pose

Ardha Uttanasana: Half forward fold

Baddha Konasana: Cobbler's pose

Balasana: Child's pose

Bhujangasana: Cobra pose

Camatkarasana: Wild thing

Chapasana: Bound half moon pose or sugarcane pose

Chaturanga Dandasana: Four limbed staff pose

Dandasana: Staff or stick pose

Eka Pada Rajakapotasana: One-legged king pigeon pose

Gomukasana: Cow face pose

Halasana: Plough pose

Janu Sirsasana: Head to knee pose

Marichyasana 1: Pose dedicated to the sage Marichi

Natarajasana: Dancer's pose

Navasana: Boat pose

Parighasana: Gate pose

Parivrtta Parsvakonasana: Revolved side angle pose

Parsvakonasana: Extended side angle pose

Paschimottanasana: West stretch or seated forward bend

Prasarita Padottanasana: Wide legged forward bend

Prone: Lying down horizontally, face down

Purvottanasana: Intense east-facing stretch

Salabhasana: Locust pose

Salamba Bhujangasana: Sphinx pose

Salamba Sirsasana: Headstand

Savasana: Corpse pose

Setu Bandha Sarvangasana: Bridge pose

Sukhasana: Easy, seated pose

Supine: Lying down horizontally, face up

Supta Padangusthasana: Reclining hand to big toe pose

Tadasana: Mountain pose

Trikonasana: Triangle pose

Urdhva Dhanurasana: Wheel pose

Urdhva Hastasana: Raised hands pose

Urdhva Mukha Svanasana: Upward facing dog

Ustrasana: Camel pose

Utkata Konasana: Goddess pose

Utkatasana: Chair pose

Uttanasana: Standing forward bend

Utthita Hasta Padangustasana: Extended hand to big toe pose

Vajrasana: Thunderbolt pose

Vashistasana B: Bound side plank pose

Vashistasana: Side plank pose

Virabhadrasana 1, 2 and 3: Warrior pose variations
Vrksasana: Tree pose

INDEX